CLASSIC TRAINS

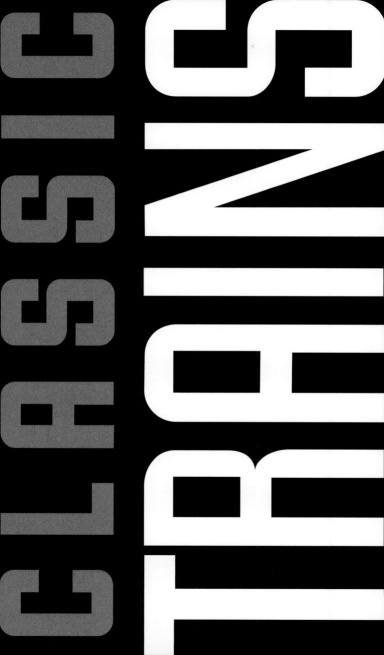

Dedication

For Justine—our own streamlined, high-powered, elegant little classic.

Library of Congress Cataloging-in-Publication Data

Halberstadt, Hans.
  Classic trains / Hans Halberstadt.
    p.cm.
  Includes bibliographical references and index.
  ISBN 1-58663-110-1
  [1. Railroads—Trains—History.] I. Title.

TF550 .H35 2001
384'.0973—dc21

2001033714

MetroBooks

An Imprint of Friedman/Fairfax Publishers

Editor: Ann Kirby-Payne
Art Director: Kevin Ullrich
Designer: Mark Weinberg
Photo Editor: Lori Epstein
Production Manager: Richela Fabian Morgan

1 3 5 7 9 10 8 6 4 2

Color separations by Fine Arts Repro House Co., Ltd.
Printed in China by C&C Offset Printing Co. Ltd

For bulk purchases and special sales, please contact:
    Friedman/Fairfax Publishers
    Attention: Sales Department
    230 Fifth Ave
    New York, NY 10001
    212/685-6610 FAX 212/685-3916

Visit our Website:
www.metrobooks.com

CONTENTS

GETTING UP STEAM

ABOVE: Yosemite Valley No. 21 is a good example of the journeyman American Class locomotive that carried everybody everywhere for many years. This particular locomotive transported passengers from California's central valley, up along the Merced River to the national park where they oohed and ahhhed at the turn of the century as much as tourists do today. Today, though, they have to drive.

OPPOSITE: Santa Fe No. 3759 pauses at San Bernardino, California, late at night with a passenger train on the drawbar. The fireman takes this opportunity to make his inspection and to "oil around." Seen here in 1952, No. 3759 is a 1928 graduate of the Baldwin Locomotive Works.

Early morning at Santa Fe's Redondo Junction roundhouse, near Los Angeles, California, 1943: Engine 3785, a huge 4-8-4 Northern-class built by Baldwin, simmers and shines under the attention of a small horde of "hostlers" who are fueling, lubricating, and wiping down the nearly new engine. Engine 3785 is the premier locomotive of Santa Fe Junction's passenger operation—powerful, fast, dependable, and very handsome—and as such gets the glamour assignments. Today, the big Northern will be "power on the point" for one of the most elegant, exclusive, and famous runs in the United States, taking the Santa Fe Super Chief—"Train of the Stars"—on its first fast leg out of Los Angeles and off toward Chicago.

The locomotive is oil-fired, and the tanks of her tender are topped off with thousands of gallons of liquid fuel and boiler feed water. Her fires have been lit for hours, warming her up, and she now has enough pressure to move out of the roundhouse, to be spotted on the outbound lead, ready for her crew.

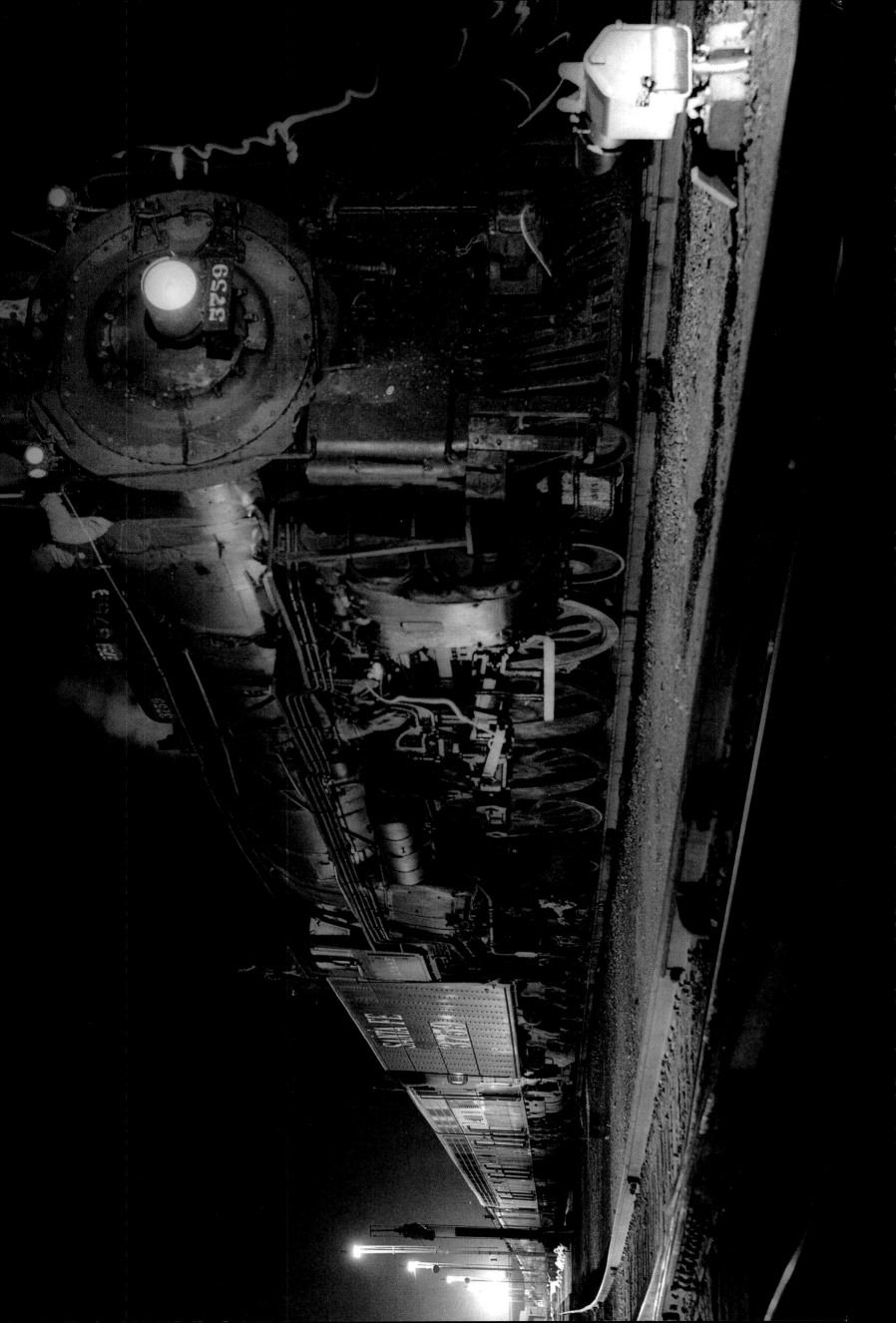

Senior Fireman Jack Elwood (who is, in fact, only twenty-three years old) gets the call at home from the crew clerk around breakfast time. A fireman without a lot of seniority will get called for everything, from a switcher in the yard, to a "dog local" freight to the grandest locomotive on the grandest run on the system. "You are called for No. 20, the Chief," the clerk on the phone says, "on duty at 11 AM at the Redondo Junction roundhouse, with Engineer J.P. Murray and Engine 3785." This is "hogger" heaven.

Elwood hustles down to the roundhouse and completes the several forms required to take custody of the locomotive. He signs the "Hours of Service" forms, enters the engineer's name and his own on the Outbound Register for Train No. 20, and then compares his watch to the synchronized official time displayed in the roundhouse office.

Now it's off to the locomotive, waiting on the outbound lead. Elwood climbs into the cab and makes his checks: boiler water between the lines in the sight glass, no visible leaks in the firebox, no cracks or dropped bricks, no other apparent problems. He adjusts the valve that controls fuel flow to the burners and opens it to get up steam. A deep, muscular roar comes from behind the cast iron firebox doors as the locomotive begins to awaken for another day.

Elwood gathers up a bundle of rags and an oiler that Engineer Murray will use on his walk-around inspection (one of his many prescribed crew duties) and sets them aside. Then he clambers up on the tender to check fuel and water levels; the locomotive will suck up 120 gallons (456L) of water for every mile going up Cajon Pass, so it is essential that the tender have full tanks. Both are topped off, as they should be, and he climbs back down into the cab.

Oil-fired locomotives get greasy when in use, so Elwood takes a hose attached to the boiler and blasts off the cab deck with high-pressure water that is boiling hot. It washes the steel plates clean and dries in an instant. Murray arrives with his gear and bag, climbs aboard and stows the grip behind his seat, then climbs back down for his inspection with the rags and oil can.

Not far away, over at the Los Angeles Union Passenger Terminal, the cars of the Super Chief await

both their power and their passengers. Aboard already are dozens of porters, stewards, barmen, cooks, and at least one maid—nearly all of them black, and nearly all of them working at one of the best paying, most prestigious jobs then available to them. Long before departure, food preparation is well underway for the evening meal by the galley crew, who are cheerfully peeling, slicing, chopping, and chatting away.

Passengers begin to arrive well before departure time. Tickets are inspected, baggage is loaded in the baggage car, and the rich and famous find their cars and their reserved compartments. The Super Chief, as befits one of the most elegant fast trains, has no chair cars; all accommodations are in private compartments. The passengers settle in, explore a bit, read *Life* or *Look* or *The Saturday Evening Post*, and wait with expectant excitement.

Over at Redondo Junction, Elwood opens the cylinder drains with a remote control in the cab, then cracks the throttle a bit, feeding steam to the massive pistons and cylinders, and bringing them up

to operating temperature. White steam and water sprays from the front of the locomotive with a roar.

Murray finishes his inspection and climbs back into the cab. He adjusts the seat to suit himself and does his first air brake check. Then he tests the sander, inspects each of his gauges, and finds no fault with anything. He reaches up, grasps the whistle cord, and gives it three short tugs—toot, toot, toot! That's the indication to the men in the tower that 3785 is ready to move.

Murray opens the throttle, washing the last of any possible condensation from the cylinders, then operates the control to close the vents. The locomotive begins to move toward the outbound track. He pulls the cord again, and the whistle blasts one long and three short. The singal indicates that the train is ready for the mainline. The switch is opened, and Murray gets his signal to proceed. Rumbling down to get the cars that will make up the rest of Train No. 20, Murray opens the boiler drains momentarily, blasting sludge and sediment onto the ballast beneath the slowly moving locomotive.

*LEFT: **Down by the lakefront at 27th Street, Illinois Central's Chicago roundhouse was a busy place in 1934, when this photograph was made. The train yard was designed for smaller locomotives and an earlier time; current residents have engineer whose duties involve moving locomotives in and out of the roundhouse. The turntable will be aligned with the house track, then No. 727 will be handed off to her assigned crew for the day's duties.***

*OPPOSITE ABOVE: **Nickel Plate Road's 727 is being moved by a "hostler," an apprentice engineer whose duties involve moving locomotives in and out of the roundhouse. The turntable will be aligned with the house track, then No. 727 will be handed off to her assigned crew for the day's duties.***

*OPPOSITE BELOW: **Union Pacific No. 3955 is a nearly new Challenger, seen here on the turntable at Cheyenne in 1944. One of the challenges for UP was finding places to turn the huge locomotive around.***

Under the watchful eye and careful control of the signal tower crew, 3785 hooks up to its assignment. The air lines that control the train's brakes are connected, then the electrical lines, followed by the steam line for the passenger car heating system.

Murray now has fourteen cars firmly attached to 3785's tender, and about a halt an hour to go before the scheduled departure. All along the train, smiling porters and attendants help elegant ladies and gentlemen climb the steps into their reserved cars, and everybody watches the clock.

It takes a few minutes for the compressor on the engine to charge the brake line. When Murray sees the pressure come up all the way, he makes a full application. Two carmen walk the length of the whole train, inspecting every brake to make sure it is engaged. When they get to the rear, they signal to the cab to "release brakes," and Murray charges the line again. The carmen walk back toward the cab, checking that each brake has been released. Murray watches the gauge and sees a minimal loss of pressure. Train No. 20, the Santa Fe Super Chief, is nearly ready for departure.

Now the conductor walks up to the cab with the train orders. All three read them together, synchronize watches, and confirm that the track out of the station is clear of incoming trains up to Broadway, where double tracking begins. Jack Elwood has been closely monitoring fuel feed, water level, and steam—now up at 300 pounds per square inch (psi), normal working pressure for 3785.

The last of the passengers scurry aboard; flustered, with seconds to spare, they find their compartments and drawing rooms while the conductor on the platform watches for even later arrivals. At the appointed moment, the conductor faces the cab, which is two hundred yards (180m) up the platform, and he raises a green flag to signal Murray out of the terminal and on toward Chicago. Murray has already released the brakes and now cracks open the throttle. The Santa Fe Super Chief is on its way.

That was in 1943, and the world has changed in many ways since. That technology, and this method of travel, has gone out of popular fashion and widely been abandoned. The glittering cars and glittering people are mostly gone today, having been replaced by younger versions.

And yet there is something about locomotives like 3785 and about trains like Santa Fe's glorious Super Chief that made a mark on our culture and heritage that doesn't seem to have entirely faded away. If anything, this heritage seems to have acquired a new life of its own, with legions of fans and magazines devoted to preserving that legacy.

America is never going to go back to the train for routine long-distance travel—private automobiles, interstate freeways, and airplanes have guaranteed that. But there seems to be a consensus that, despite all the seeming advantages of cars and planes and freeways, for many Americans, travel by train during the decades between about 1920 and about 1955 was unsurpassed by anything available to us today—at any cost. That was the epoch of the Twentieth Century Limited, Pan American, Zephyr, Hiawatha, Broadway Limited, Daylights, and so many more—the golden, gilded, glorious era of the classic trains.

Chapter One

THE EARLY YEARS

A s with so many other things American, the origins of U.S. railroading began in Britain. The first practical locomotives were demonstrated in England as early as 1804, and by the late 1820s, steam locomotives were hauling passengers and freight along many miles of well-constructed track.

Railroads were in use in the United States, but they were powered by horses, and the rails were generally flimsy affairs of wooden beams with a strip of iron attached to the top. But there was growing interest and excitement about the potential of steam power as practiced by the British, and plans to adapt it for use on the lightweight rails already in place.

The first locomotive of any kind to operate in America was, naturally, a British import. This capable little tea kettle was named the *Stourbridge Lion*. The engine was purchased for use on the Delaware and Hudson Canal Company's track in Pennsylvania. The locomotive arrived in May 1829, and was assembled and tested on two occasions in August and September of that year. The locomotive worked well enough, but the track was simply too flimsy to support its weight. The locomotive derailed on both occasions and was stored in a shed, abandoned as a failure.

OPPOSITE: *Massive cast iron components provide considerable durability for old locomotives, like the drivers of Chicago & North Western No. 1385, but their bulk and weight make repairs extremely difficult, with specialized facilities and fixtures required.*

ABOVE: *While American locomotives were taking their first baby steps, British versions were being refined and perfected into practical machines. This is George Stephenson's legendary Rocket, built in 1829 in England.*

"Tom Thumb" and Other Little Engines that Could

The potential of steam power lured many inventors and business interests, and new trials with new locomotives popped up all over place. One of these came from the fertile mind of Peter Cooper, a jack of all trades and a master of most. Cooper built a light little engine in 1829 to demonstrate the practicality of steam on American rails and tested it on the tracks of the Baltimore & Ohio (B&O).

This diminutive engine had an upright boiler which measured about 18 or 20 inches (45.72cm or 50.8cm) in diameter and about 5 feet (1.5m) high ("about the size of a flour barrel," Cooper would later recall), and leaked steam from its seams. Its tubes were old gun barrels, the only suitable tubes readily available to Cooper at the time. Connected to a crankshaft was a small piston and cylinder with a tiny 3.25-inch (8.26cm) and 14-inch (35.56cm) stroke. Instead of using exhaust steam to increase draft as demonstrated in England, Cooper's little engine used a fan driven by a belt, an important feature because the engine was fired with difficult-to-burn anthracite coal. Its driving wheels were only about 2 feet (60.96cm) in diameter with beveled-bearing surfaces, unlike the flat form on English engines, to better keep the locomotive on the track. The engine produced about one horsepower.

The whole package was experimental and only intended to show that steam power was superior to horses and that a locomotive could negotiate tight curves; it worked on both counts. On Saturday, August 28, 1830, this little locomotive was attached to a carriage stuffed with twenty-eight passengers, and departed from Pratt Street in Baltimore on a trial run to Ellicott's Mills, 13 miles (20.92km) away.

The route ran through steep, rocky terrain, with grades of 15 feet (4.57m) to the mile and many sharp turns. The first mile was completed in about seven minutes; the second in just five—a thrilling 12 miles per hour (19.2kph), Cooper's little machine huffed and puffed and made it all the way in an hour and fifteen minutes, then came back in an hour. The skeptics (well, some of them, at least) were convinced, and railroading became a much more serious proposition. At the time, this little teapot was known as the *Peter Cooper,* but much later was re-christened, in the legend and lore of railroading, the *Tom Thumb.*

Naturally, with such an important and seminal event, there is a little doubt about what actually took place on that dim and distant day. Peter Cooper, years later, described a race between his locomotive and a horse-drawn wagon on a parallel track. In one report, the belt driving the blower fan slipped, and Cooper lost the pickup race; in another version, Cooper gleefully claimed in a speech that he beat the horse. But there was no doubt that his little engine was no more than a technology demonstrator, and not intended for regular service.

Very soon, British locomotives were being imported and put to work on freshly installed rails. A spiderweb of iron and steel began to form a network across the eastern United States, connecting cities and towns with steam-powered locomotives.

*LEFT: **Here Pullman's first lounge car is pictured in all its glittering 1882 glory. Note the upholstered chairs, fine woodwork, and brass fixtures; this is the epitome of Victorian elegance.***

*ABOVE: **An early advertisement for the Baltimore & Ohio Railroad.***

*OPPOSITE: **This reconstruction of the pioneer locomotive later known as Tom Thumb is based on guesswork and the recollections of Peter Cooper many years after its first epic journey. According to Cooper, its vertical tubes were made of old gun barrels, and the boiler shell was about the size of a flour barrel.***

BALTIMORE & OHIO R.R.

THE ROAD TO WASHINGTON

Best Friend of Charleston

One of the first locomotives and the official granddaddy of serious American engines was the *Best Friend of Charleston*. Generally considered the first steam locomotive to pull a train, this engine was a remarkable success. Designed and built in New York's West Point Foundry and shipped down the coast on a sailing vessel, *Best Friend of Charleston* made a trial run in November 1830, and made its official debut on Christmas Day of that same year, establishing North America's first regularly scheduled passenger train service. The *Charleston Courier* described that maiden voyage on December 29: "The one hundred and forty-one persons flew on the wings of wind at the speed of 15 to 25 miles per hour [24.16 to 40.23 kph], annihilating time and space . . . leaving all the world behind."

In another first, *Best Friend of Charleston* made history in June 1831, when its uneducated and inexperienced fireman became annoyed with the noise of steam escaping from the safety valve and held its lever down. The steam pressure built up in the boiler, and it exploded, killing the fireman and injuring the engineer in what is widely regarded as the Americas' first railroading disaster. The *Best Friend* was destroyed, only to move on to another first: within three years, it had been reconstructed and put back on the rails, the first locomotive ever to be rebuilt after such a catastrophe. The new locomotive that rose from the *Best Friend's* ashes was aptly named *The Phoenix*.

A full-size replica of the *Best Friend of Charleston* was constructed in 1928 from the original plans, in commemoration of the South Carolina Canal and Rail Road Company's centennial. Norfolk Southern donated the engine to the city of Charleston in 1993, and today that replica—now nearly an antique in its own right—is housed in the city's *Best Friend of Charleston Museum*.

RIGHT: **The Best Friend of Charleston was the first American locomotive to have much real success. Here it is, 129 years after its triumph, at the Chicago Railroad Fair of 1949.**

RAILROAD ECONOMICS 101

Competition was brutal during the entire railroad era, and the early railroads had to account for every penny spent if they were to survive. The accountants were relentless in chasing down every cost and calculating it into their annual reports. As a result, we have a pretty good idea of what it cost to own and operate one of these handsome little American locomotives almost from the beginning of the industry.

For sixty years, from 1843 until the first years of the twentieth century, the price of an American-class locomotive stayed right around ten thousand dollars, even though the size, complexity, and technological development of the engine increased substantially. Wood was the preferred fuel and a whole industry developed to supply it to the railroads at anything from one dollar to eight dollars per cord, each cord propelling a standard train about 40 miles (64.36km).

The engineers of these pretty little locomotives received about two or two and a half dollars a day; their firemen usually half that, and the daring brakemen who jumped from one car roof to the next, who died and were maimed by the thousands every year, got one dollar a day. The conductor got two dollars a day. In total, contemporary accountants found that it cost about twenty-five cents per mile to operate a conventional locomotive in conventional service during the 1870s.

LEFT: *Travel by rail may have been the height of elegance for Victorian travelers, but fierce competition between railroads kept operating budgets lean. Virtually every penny—from porters' salaries to the cost of fuel—had to be accounted for.*

17

CHAPTER TWO

CLASSIC LOCOMOTIVE TYPES

OPPOSITE: The US government took over control of much railroad administration during World War One, including the design of locomotives. This K-5 is a heavy Pacific engine built to US Railroad Administration specifications in 1919. It was still hard at work twenty-five years later, accelerating toward the camera with a heavy trailing load in 1944.

ABOVE: New York Central's No. 567 is a fine example of the American Standard pattern, and a classic locomotive. Its four driving wheels and four leading wheels on a swiveling truck provided excellent traction and stability on the rough track of its day, just after the Civil War.

R ailroading in the United States, like so many other American institutions, was a British import, which was modified, adjusted, and customized for a different landscape. The steam engine and the steam locomotive both originated in England and found their early development there, before they were adopted in America. Steam-powered trains were in revenue service in Britain well before the first little engine, the *Stourbridge Lion*, was imported and tested here in 1829. The engine would have worked well enough had its American owners used something besides lightweight wooden rails made from hemlock. The weight of the little locomotive (about six tons) was too much for the rails, and it was almost instantly put in storage, then consigned to scrap—although its British twin labored faithfully and efficiently for three decades in the same service for which the *Stourbridge Lion* had been intended.

The *John Bull*, the next noteworthy import, arrived in 1832, and was more successful. This little machine worked all kinds of trains—freight, passenger, and construction—

4-4-0 "American Standard" Locomotive

An American Standard-class (normally called just American-class) uses a four-wheel forward truck and four driving wheels supporting the firebox and rear of the boiler. The forward truck is mounted on a swivel, a modification to the original English design that adapted the machine to American roadbeds and their tight curves. The first of these, built in the 1840s, weighed about eighteen tons, burned wood, and had a tractive force of around 4,500 pounds (2,043kg). Their cabs were still open, in the British style, but their frames were inside the driving wheels and cylinders, making them already a new breed entirely. Their tender could supply a cord of wood and about 1,000 gallons (3,800L) of boiler feed water. According to John White's book, *The History of the American Locomotive*, these early American-class 4-4-0s produced about 240 horsepower at 20 miles per hour (32.18kph).

Twenty years later, the same wheel pattern and general layout remained standard, but at about double the size—tractive force was now up to almost 10,000 pounds (4,540kg). locomotive weight up to thirty tons, and tender capacity up to 2,000 gallons (7,600L) of boiler feed water and two cords of wood. American-class locomotives would continue to be built into the twentieth century, long after bigger and more powerful designs became popular, and they con-

tinued in revenue service for more than a hundred years. The reason for this longevity was that they were an inherently durable machine when used as intended—at slow speeds, carrying light loads, and routinely maintained.

Properly cared for, these locomotives lasted almost forever; 30,000 miles (48,000km) of revenue service per year was routine around the time of the Civil War, and double that ten years later. Year after year, each engine accumulated as much as a million miles of service before being scrapped. Later, more powerful and complex engines would not last nearly so long or prove so reliable.

Wood was the primary fuel for locomotives until well after the Civil War, even though

for the Camden & Amboy Railroad until being honorably retired twenty-six years later in 1858, when it was preserved for posterity. By that dim and distant year, American locomotive design had long since evolved into something entirely different from the original British designs. Roadbeds in England were much smoother and straighter, and distances traveled were

typically much shorter than those in the United States. American roadbeds were rough, ragged affairs, constructed in haste with tight curves and steep grades. The locomotive developed in response to that rough and rocky terrain was a pattern that would serve well and faithfully for over half a century, a basic design called the American Standard.

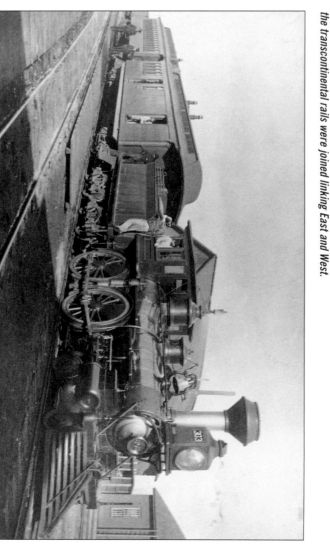

OPPOSITE BOTTOM: *New York Central's No. 1003 approaches the water tower for a fill-up sometime in 1896.*

ABOVE: *Here comes a very important little train—the Pennsylvania Railroad's pay car, pulled by No. 929, a Class D13a version of the old 4-4-0 American Standard, built in June of 1891.*

coal was abundant. The problem with coal was that it was much more difficult to burn and required an entirely different—and larger—firebox for proper combustion. That firebox would come, along with much bigger engines, after the war.

American-class 4-4-0 engines built the whole railroading tradition in the United States and captured the imagination of the public. Even today, the form of the typical 4-4-0 locomotives, (like the two that connected the coasts at Promontory, Utah, in 1869, the *Jupiter* and Union Pacific (UP) No. 119), seems perfect—nicely proportioned, elegant, richly detailed, and just the right size. Extensive use of brass was standard, as was the use of furniture-grade hardwoods in the cab—cherry, oak, walnut—beautifully finished, varnished, and embellished with ornamental paintings executed by skilled craftsmen.

Later, locomotives would lose the gaudy paint schemes and gold leaf, the huge square headlights and massive spark-arresting funnels. With them they lost a bit of their appeal, too.

ABOVE: **Commodore Vanderbilt must have been quite proud of his own glittering locomotive, seen here in all its new glory. It is a typical example of the American Standard 4-4-0 built in the years following the Civil War—a time when you could run a train down the middle of the street.**

4-6-0 "Ten Wheeler" Locomotive

American-class 4-4-0 locomotives dominated the rails all across the country for fifty years for several good reasons, one of which was that they would stay on the rails no matter how badly laid and maintained the roadbeds were. But the limitations of that little format prevented very much growth, and more power was something that was in great demand by all railroads after the Civil War.

An additional set of drivers allowed a longer boiler and better steaming capability, and another set of wheels ensured improved traction. The concept was offered for the first time by the Norris shops in 1847 by way of a capable engine named the *Chesapeake*. This prototype ten-wheeler was destined to the grimy job of hauling coal cars, one hundred at a time, but did it so well that its new owners, the Philadelphia & Reading Railroad, sent Norris a letter of appreciation for its several excellent features.

The ten-wheeler was an idea waiting for realization, and Norris had a lot of competiton for the heavy-hauler locomotive market. American-class engines were still the favorite for primitive roadbeds but the ten-wheeler soon became the choice for heavy trailing loads and slow speeds.

LEFT: Northern Pacific No. 328 carefully crosses the tightrope across the St. Croix River with a short string of passenger cars. About one hundred steam locomotives, like this durable ten-wheeler built by Rogers in 1907, provide occasional steam-powered thrills for railfans around the United States and Canada.

Many ten-wheelers are still in business around the United States—Nevada Northern's No. 40, Osceola & St. Croix Valley Railway's No. 328, Milwaukee Road's No. 261, and Union Pacific's No. 1243, among others. Union Pacific's No. 1243 is a good example of this honorable clan—built in 1890, it labored on Nebraska's prairies for over forty years before reassignment to Wyoming. Union Pacific put 1243 out to pasture in 1956 after a career three or four times longer than most steam locomotives.

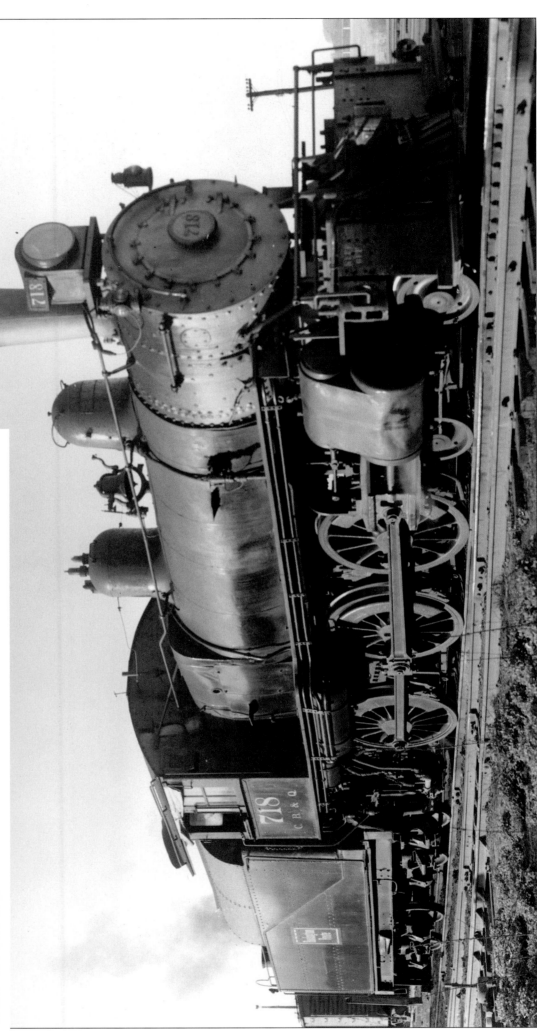

OPPOSITE: **Chicago & North Western No. 328.** *Ten-wheelers like this were the most popular locomotive on American rails in the late nineteenth century, right after the 4-4-0 American Standard.*

ABOVE: **Here are a brace of ten-wheelers being prepared for delivery at the Brooks Locomotive Works for the Lake Shore & Michigan Southern. The large-diameter wheels and glossy paint job suggest these will pull passenger trains.**

RIGHT: **CB&Q No. 718** *is a well-worn little ten-wheeler late in life. It is a K-10 variant, one of nineteen, the last of which was retired in 1953.*

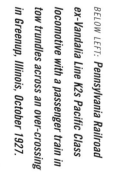

4-6-2 "Pacific" Locomotive

Locomotives with four wheels on a leading truck, six drivers, and two at the rear supporting the firebox are known as Pacifics, another classic design. Essentially a variant of the 4-4-2 Atlantic, the Pacific offered extra traction and extra power from a bigger boiler and firebox.

Although locomotives with this basic layout were built in the 1880s, the early trials were not very successful. Only with a Baldwin design delivered in 1901 did this basic breed begin to show its potential, and that was for a railroad in New Zealand.

Brooks Locomotive Works delivered the first American model the following year, and the Chesapeake & Ohio produced a variant of its own, designated F15 4-6-2 Pacific-class.

Pacifics aren't—and weren't then—the biggest kids on the block, but they combined many excellent qualities that quickly made them a favorite basic design. Fireboxes were deep and wide, allowing efficient conversion of coal to steam at a rapid rate, and that translated to a kind of cast-iron agility: plenty of speed and the ability to accelerate quickly when required. These fireboxes were typically around

50 feet square (15.24m²), which left plenty of grate surface for a nice cozy fire.

Of the many surviving and steaming classic Pacifics, Southern Pacific's 2472 is a great example of the best of the breed. Built in 1921 by Baldwin, 2472 was one of fifteen P-7 variants ordered by Southern Pacific (SP) and put into service hauling all kinds of

trains, both passenger and freight. It is about 90 feet (27.43m) long, including tender, and weighs over 2,700,000 pounds (1,225,800kg). Boiler pressure is 210 pounds (95.34kg), feeding two cylinders with 25-inch (63.5cm) bore and 30-inch (76.2cm) stroke.

This handsome locomotive was spared by SP and put on static display in a fairground where kids climbed

all over it, vandals smashed whatever they could, and it was generally allowed to rot. But beginning in 1976, a group of volunteers went to work on the hulk and began to put it back in working condition. That took fifteen years, but 2472 came back to life after a thirty-year sleep in 1991. It has been used for excursions and has recently undergone another extensive rebuild.

Southern Pacific's Cab-Forwards

American railroading is loaded with variety. There are all sorts of big locomotives, small locomotives, and strange locomotives. Among the latter class, beloved by a special group of western railfans, is Southern Pacific's curious "cab-forwards."

The western slope of the Sierra Nevada mountains is steep, rugged, and covered with snow for many months of the year. Building a railroad across it was a monumental challenge in the 1860s, and keeping a railroad in operation across this region has been a challenge ever since.

The railroad spanned Southern Pacific's Sacramento Division, between Roseville, just east of Sacramento, up and over the crest 150 miles (241.35km) to Sparks, Nevada. With grades of up to

250 feet (76.2m) to the mile and roadbeds that were Lally-blasted out of the sides of mountains, it was and is a difficult place to run a train. The use of snowplows is a fine art on this division, and were it not for many miles of snow sheds—a kind of man-made tunnel to keep the snow off the track—travel up here would be exclusively a summertime thing.

Any "hogger" running a train over this division spends about 20 percent of his or her time in a tunnel or shed, 30 miles (48.27km) worth between either end of the division. In the days of steam with conventional locomotives, the tunnel time resulted in a well-smoked hogger because all the smoke from the locomotive was funneled back toward the cab. Engineers and firemen on the up-grades were nearly

asphyxiated by the fumes, and the passengers didn't do much better.

Southern Pacific came up with a way to keep their crews from choking on the smoke by turning the locomotives around and putting the cab toward the front. This configuration makes the crew much more vulnerable in a grade-crossing collision, but there are few of these crossings on the Sacramento Division anyway.

Mallets are "compound" locomotives, essentially two locomotives sharing one gigantic boiler, with a frame that is hinged to allow its ponderous bulk to get around curves. The front low-pressure pair of cylinders in a normal Mallet recycle the steam used by the rear high-pressure pair, a design that was

ABOVE: Another of SP's Baldwin-built cab-forwards, No. 4164 was built in 1937. With the tender far behind the firebox, the only way to fuel these locomotives was with oil, pumped through a pipe along the boiler, instead of coal.

LEFT: These 4-8-8-4 compounds were developed to deal with the extensive snow sheds and tunnels on SP's Sacramento District, over the Sierras, but they worked equally well in the Siskiou Mountains of northern California. This one has halted at the little railroad town of Dunsmuir, California, in June of 1945.

BELOW: *Eastbound from Oakland, Southern Pacific (SP)'s No. 4220 rolls onto the Carquinez Strait Bridge near Martinez, California, with a mixed freight. 4220 is one of SP's curious "cab-forwards." It will skirt the vast Sacramento River delta, then begin the long pull up into the Sierras, through Roseville, over the crest near Truckee, and down into Reno.*

complicated but attractive when it first appeared in 1904.

SP ordered a pair of new locomotives from Baldwin, a hybrid Mallet-Consolidation design, in 1908 and sent them up the hill to Sparks. The engineers and firemen were smoked "hoggers," and the exhaust from the stack blew the planks right off the snow sheds. The crews couldn't see forward because of the smoke, even when they were holding their breath. Southern Pacific designated these MC-1s, which stood for Mallet-Consolidation, version one.

Despite the crew problems, the locomotives had the power SP wanted, and so SP turned their design staff loose on the difficulty. The result was simple enough—they just turned the locomotives around

and added exhaust deflectors to the stack. The tender stayed where it belonged, though, so the fuel oil for the boiler was pumped through pipes alongside the boiler up to the firebox at the front. SP ordered fifteen without even testing a prototype. These had headlights and cowcatchers on the cab, instead of at the opposite end of the locomotive, and were designated MC-2s.

The result of all this was a locomotive that looked odd but worked very well for its unusual application. SP bought 256 cab-forwards over the years, worked them hard, then cut them all up for scrap, the last in 1960 . . . except for one, SP No. 4294, now restored and on static display at the California State Railroad Museum in Sacramento.

BALDWIN LOCOMOTIVE WORKS

Of all the many designers and builders of American steam locomotives, the one that blew the proverbial doors off the competition was the Baldwin Locomotive Works, the Ford Motor Company of the industry. Beginning at the very dawn of American steam railroading, Baldwin was founded in 1831 in Philadelphia, Pennsylvania, by its namesake, Matthias Baldwin.

Baldwin's first locomotive looked like a toy, and that's essentially what it was—a little engine that was set up indoors on a tiny track, with tiny coaches, that pulled a few delighted people in circles. But its purpose was serious, to demonstrate that smooth wheels and smooth rails and steam power were all compatible, and in this it succeeded.

Like other American builders in the 1830s and 1840s, Baldwin turned out engines that looked very much like their English cousins—outside frames, exposed platforms—simple little concoctions with a single pair of drivers, small cylinders, and a sticker price of $5,500 out the door, tender included.

Baldwin dominated the American market with a combination of excellent design, generally flawless fit and finish, and competitive prices. During the Civil War, Baldwin churned out locomotives as fast as they could get the raw materials to build them, an average of around 150 a year. Toward the end of the nineteenth century, that rate went up to well over six hundred locomotives annually, about a third of all domestic production. Early in the twentieth century, Baldwin employed over eighteen thousand men and was one of the leading industrial operations in the nation.

Over the years, Baldwin produced all kinds of steam locomotives, from little yard switchers to massive 2-8-8-2 compounds. The company was adept at producing exotic specialized designs like SP's unusual cab-forwards. Baldwin's Mikados and Northerns were well-regarded and ordered by many railroads in wholesale quantities. But, like so many others in the American railroad industry, the conversion to diesel-electrics was a cruel one, and Baldwin faded out of the business. Their last steam locomotive was fabricated in 1956.

ABOVE: Baldwin's 2-8-2 Mikado was a popular steam locomotive that was ordered in large numbers by several railroads. This profile of the Chicago Burlington & Quincy No. 5116 reveals the classic lines of locomotive and tender.

LEFT: By World War II, the quest for motive power steam technology had reached amazing extremes. This is Baldwin's first experimental rigid frame duplex locomotive—a 4-4-4-4 built for Pennsylvania Railroad in 1942

LEFT: In the post–World War II period, Baldwin became a specialist in huge steam locomotives, like this 1945 Baltimore & Ohio EM-1.

BELOW: The Baldwin diesels known as "Sharks" for their distinctive profiles were common sights on the New York Central, Pennsylvania, and Baltimore & Ohio railroads. No. 6001 was a demonstrator unit that eventually went to the B&O.

4-8-4 Northern Locomotives

One of the most successful locomotive designs of all time, and one still seen in operation today, is the big 4-8-4 Northern-class. First developed in the 1920s, the first Northern-class was delivered from the American Locomotive Works in late 1926 and was an immediate hit. Unlike most other locomotives, the 4-8-4 has a lot of aliases—it has been occasionally called the Confederation (in Canada), Wyoming, Potomac, Niagara, and Pocono during its long years of service—but Northern is the name used today, a tip of the hat to the Northern Pacific Railroad, source of the first order for the big engine.

It's a big machine, able to cruise at 100 miles per hour (160.9kph) or pull a trailing load of several thousand tons—though not both at the same time. The four-wheel trailing truck supports a big firebox, and that firebox generates a lot of heat for the boiler.

Union Pacific's 844 is a typical example of the best of the breed—198 tubes in the boiler, each 2 1/4 inches (5.72cm) in diameter, and designed to operate at 300 pounds-per-inch. UP 844's cylinders are as big as trash cans, 25 inches (63.5cm) by 32 inches (81.28cm). It is 114 feet (34.75m) long, including the tender, and weighs about 908,000 pounds (412,232kg). It was a stable, powerful, reliable, and reasonably economical locomotive with a design that lasted in revenue service long after most other designs had been butchered by the scrapper's cutting torch.

Between 1926 and 1950, when the last one was produced for Norfolk & Western, over a thousand Northerns were built and put in service. Seven of these Northerns, amazingly, are still in some degree of operation: SP 4449, Norfolk Western 611, Milwaukee Road 261, Chesapeake & Ohio 614, Santa Fe 3751, and UP 844.

Southern Pacific operated a lot of Northerns, mainly GS-4 variants, on its premier passenger runs, the Daylights, and later in commuter service on the San Francisco peninsula well into the 1950s. SP 4449 is one of these, and a survivor.

Originally built by Lima Locomotive Works in the early 1940s, 4449 is an oil-burner and equipped with all the bells and whistles available from Lima at the time. These include a fuel economy gauge, electro-pneumatic brakes, an oversize sand reservoir, and three turbo-generators.

Union Pacific's 844 has never been retired and has occasionally thrilled railfans patrolling out West with the sight of this grand old locomotive on the point of a long string of freight cars.

Norfolk AND Western RAILWAY

N & W Streamliners Speed
Through All Kinds of Weather

Time Tables

January 20, 1946—No. 1

PRECISION TRANSPORTATION

ABOVE LEFT: Baldwin built a lot of locomotives for Santa Fe, including this stalwart Northern, SF No. 2907, entering the East Switch above the fabled Cajon Pass north of Los Angeles sometime in 1952. The locomotive was built in 1943, just one of a litter of thirty similar engines, the last of which was cut up in 1959.

ABOVE: A 1946 time table for the Norfolk and Western railway boasted "precision transportation."

LEFT: Locomotives like this one with four leading wheels, eight drivers, and four supporting the firebox have generally been known as Northern types, but some railroads insisted on calling them Niagaras or other names. This one is "power on the point" for The Chicagoan shortly after World War II. Those sheet metal panels at the front of the boiler are smoke deflectors, often called "elephant ears."

LIMA LOCOMOTIVE WORKS

Lima Locomotive Works came late to the business of locomotive building, but they learned fast and became one of the big three. Originally known as the Lima Machine Works of Lima, Ohio, the company was organized in 1869 and made farm machinery until commissioned to make an innovative little logging locomotive using the design by Ephraim Shay in the early 1890s. That little backwoods locomotive was just the ticket for the then-booming lumber industry, and Shay engines sold like hotcakes.

Lima started competing with Baldwin and the rest of the established builders in a serious way around 1900, with small switchers and logging engines. Around the time of the beginning of World War I, that business expanded to mainline locomotives for the major railroads. The company prospered during and immediately after the war, churning out excellent and innovative engines for faithful customers like the New York Central.

The company's masterpiece, the 2-8-4 Berkshire, was a quick, powerful, and fuel-efficient design that debuted in 1920. This locomotive was designed to burn more fuel more efficiently. Its firebox had a surface area approximately 100 square feet (30.48m²), enough to keep up steam pressure under adverse conditions—high speed, steep grades, large trailing loads—and was better than anything else then available. While the general layout was known as a Berkshire type, Lima saw it as the beginning of a dynasty and designated it accordingly—the A-1.

Lima's new locomotive sold to many railroads with extensive freight operations, and was quite popular. Over six hundred were built by Lima, and the last was in service until the 1960s.

OPPOSITE: The erecting floor at Lima Locomotive Works was a busy place in 1915, with orders for locomotives large and small. That trio in the corner, No. 1701, 1702, and probably 1703, are likely to serve as switchers. In the foreground are the frames and boilers, not yet married, for more muscular machines.

ABOVE: Lima was one of the Big Three of American locomotive manufacturing and employed a huge force of highly skilled machinists and mechanics. One of them is using a specialized tool mounted on a fixture to bore out the cylinder of a locomotive.

ABOVE RIGHT: The Virginian Railway was built around the coal hauling business, and business was good with big Berkshire locomotives like No. 505. Built by the Lima Locomotive Works, and shown here in its builder portrait from 1946, No. 505 has 69-inch drivers and, according to George Drury's Guide to North American Steam Locomotives, holds the speed record for the type—87mph (140kph) with a 3500 ton trailing load.

*RIGHT: **Chesapeake & Ohio's newly minted No. 2744 is another Lima product, produced in 1944.***

Hudson Locomotive

Hudson locomotives and the 4-6-4 format appeared late in the game, in 1927. The first was ordered by the New York Central (NYC), and they named it to commemorate their lovely Hudson River route. This classic locomotive design was an extention of the Pacific-class 4-6-2, but with a bigger trailing truck to support a bigger firebox.

New York Central's program was the result of some experimentation; a plain-vanilla Pacific K-3 variant was modified with a four-wheel trailing truck and used for trials. One prototype 4-6-4 of the proposed new design was ordered from the American Locomotive Company (ALCO). It was delivered in 1927 and performed well in tests. NYC ordered fifty-nine more, the start of a fleet that would soon number 225, then 275. The Hudson locomotive was a big hit along the Hudson River. The New York Central owned most of the examples of this handsome clan delivered in the United States.

Santa Fe, Chicago & North Western (C&NW), Milwaukee Road, and Canadian Pacific (CP) all bought Hudson locomotives. Canadian Pacific bought sixty-five in the years before World War II. One of these, British Columbia Rail No. 2860, is still in daily operation during the summer on a run from Vancouver, British Columbia, up to the little tourist town of Squamish.

*ABOVE: The **New York Central** bought a lot of Hudson-class locomotives, and this is the very first, No. 5200, on its birthday in February 1927. It is the prototype of a design that would become quite successful, particularly for passenger operations. The NYC bought 275 of them over the years, in several variants.*

LEFT: Another handsome Hudson, ready to go.

OPPOSITE: The "Nickel Plate Road" was merely an alias for the New York, Chicago & St. Louis Railroad, a subsidiary of the New York Central specializing in fast freight service. Nickel Plate bought Hudsons, too, and their first batch of four were delivered right after the New York Central got their first delivery. This one is equipped with "elephant ears" smoke lifters.

This run is along the beautiful Howe Sound, and reservations are required for anyone wanting to ride behind this handsome Hudson.

CP's Hudsons are pretty good examples of the breed. Although there are some variations between them, 2860 is typical: 90 feet (27.4m) long, including tender, 15 feet (4.57m) high, with tall 75-inch (190.5cm) drivers. This Hudson weighs 675,500 pounds (306,677kg), is oil fired, and operates at 275 psi. Its firebox is quite large, about 80 square feet (24.38m²), and is nearly as broad as the locomotive itself.

All of CP's Hudsons shared these basic mechanical specifications, but they got prettier over the years.

The first were just typical steam locomotives, black and often grimy. The second batch of forty-five got a shiny steel jacket and a bit of streamlining. But the last got a very sleek treatment, with maroon paint, white wheels, and gold trim.

These last were the pride of the CP fleet, so when King George VI visited Canada in 1939, one of these Hudsons powered the royal train. Repainted in royal blue and embellished with a crown on each footboard, CP No. 2850 carried the royal party all the way across Canada. This locomotive and the coaches used by King George VI and his party all survive—the engine in the Railway Museum in Quebec, the coaches in the National Science Museum in Ottawa.

ABOVE: *The fluted stainless steel shrouding on the Chicago, Burlington & Quincy's No. 4000 locomotive (and tender) transformed the Baldwin-built 4-6-4 into a sleek, aerodynamic charger. It was named Aeolus after the Greek god of the winds, but CB&Q workers called it "Big Alice the Goon."*

LEFT: *Steam locomotive cabs are normally grimy, oily places, but this one is brand new and freshly painted. It is the interior of the CB&Q's No. 4001, an S4A Hudson built in 1938.*

AMERICAN LOCOMOTIVE COMPANY (ALCO)

RIGHT: *This 2-8-2 Mikado was built for the Missouri Pacific Lines.*

BELOW: *Deep inside ALCO's erecting shop, a "Big Boy" locomotive is carefully assembled on a hot September day in 1941. Big Boys were the real heavyweights of the steam age, 4-8-4 compounds designed for Union Pacific's heavy freights and steep grades. It would be many more years before a single diesel locomotive could equal the drawbar power of this amazing piece of cast iron technology.*

Eight small but capable locomotive builders joined forces in 1901 as the American Locomotive Company (ALCO) to compete more effectively with the giant of the day, Baldwin. These included Schenectady Locomotive Works, Brooks Locomotive Works, Cooke Locomotive and Machine Works, and several others, and were joined later by Rogers Locomotive Works and Montreal's Locomotive & Machine Company. This new company became a powerhouse and innovator during the rest of the steam-powered age, and for a while, as a diesel locomotive builder.

ALCO companies produced more than seventy-five thousand locomotives over the years before and after the merger, including many special examples. Among these are the Sandusky (made in 1837 by Rogers) and the Hiawatha (one of the first streamliners). ALCO also became a specialist at constructing the complex three-cylinder, high-power freight locomotives. Among ALCO's famous products are New York Central's Hudsons and 4-8-4 Northerns (ALCO perversely called them "Niagaras.") The company was also a favorite of Union Pacific (UP) Railroad during the late steam dynasty and helped conceive and deliver the incredible 4-8-8-4 Big Boys and 4-6-6-4 Challengers.

The vast bulk of ALCO's products came from its Schenectady, New York facilities, and they were legion: the first Mallet 0-6-6-0 locomotives in 1904, hordes of Pacific-class engines, fast freight 4-8-2 Mohawks for New York Central, and the first little diesel-electric switcher in 1924. ALCO made lots of Hudsons for lots of railroads, and its crowning glory, UP's bigger than big, 7,000-horsepower Big Boys.

Although ALCO helped pioneer the diesel-electric locomotive, General Motors and General Electric designs dominated the market, and ALCO finally went out of commission, just like its steam-powered products.

Challenger

For many reasons, the grand old Union Pacific (UP) is a remarkable railroad. Its history is synonymous with railroading in the West, from the very beginnings right up to the present. No other American railroad preserves, protects, and defends its heritage the way UP does. Witness the last working mainline steam locomotive, the glorious Challenger locomotive Union Pacific 3985. This huge locomotive is the last of the fire-breathing dragons of legend and lore still to be seen powering railfan excursions and, incredibly, occasional freight trains.

Challengers were developed to get heavy freights over the worst grades on UP territory, Utah's Wasatch Mountains. UP had been "double-heading" 2-8-8-0s and 2-10-2s, but the available locomotives weren't up to the challenge. UP had a bigger locomotive, the gigantic 4-12-0, but it was a rigid design unsuited to the mountainous roadbed. Beginning in 1934, UP and ALCO began work on a modification of that immense locomotive with four massive 22-inch (55.88cm) bore by 32-inch (81.28cm) stroke cylinders coupled to two sets of six driving wheels. With boiler pressure of 255 to 280 psi, a bigger firebox and a set of trailing wheels to support the bigger box, these locomotives were big in every way except perhaps their driving wheels, compact at 69 inches (175.26cm), Challengers are "articulated," or hinged amidships, to permit the frame of the locomotive to adapt to curved sections of track.

UP took delivery of the first one in August 1936. Challenger was sent out on the mainline for a test run from Ogden, Utah, out to Green River, Wyoming, and back, without helpers or double-heading. From that challenging run the name of the new locomotive was inspired.

The Challenger was a great success story in the closing years of steam. Over 250 were built for eight different railroads. UP bought 105 Challengers, but others went to the Western Pacific, Northern Pacific, Denver & Rio Grande Western, Western Maryland, and others.

Even though the Challengers had the muscle to perform the job for which they were bred, they proved to be a challenge to keep in service. At almost 122 feet (37.19m) long, they couldn't fit in most roundhouses. And at a weight of over a million pounds (545,000kg), they were too heavy for some bridges.

UP 3985 was built in 1943, the last year of production, and worked in revenue service for fourteen years before being retired. While the rest of the breed went off to scrap, 3985 and one other Challenger were preserved by UP and put on display. In 1981, a group of UP employees volunteered to put 3985 back in commission, and after a long period of rehabilitation, it got up steam once again. It has been extremely popular with railfan tours, and its forays out on the main line bring out the hardcore steam fans, who chase it all across the West, snapping photographs.

OPPOSITE: Union Pacific's No. 3985, seen here at Portola, California, during a railfan excursion in 1992, is a 4-6-6-4 Challenger. The UP has been the leader in preserving American rail history and heritage, with an extensive and expensive steam program. This locomotive was restored with volunteer labor by UP employees.

ABOVE: Northern Pacific put Big Boys to work, too, including NP No. 5100, seen here at rest in September 1952.

RIGHT: Union Pacific's No. 3808 was a huge 4-6-6-4 Challenger built in Schenectady during August of 1936. With a highly successful design, more than 250 of them were built between 1936 and 1943.

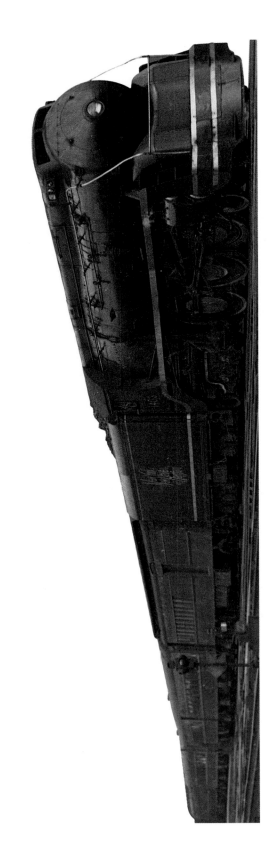

CHAPTER THREE

CLASSIC PASSENGER LINES

Almost everyone in the United States was astonished when, on May 10, 1869, the rails of the Union Pacific Railroad and those from the Central Pacific met and were joined at a remote little hillside in Promontory, Utah. It was one of those things that people said couldn't be done, and it was finished in a bit more than three years of incredible vision, persistence, effort, and money—most of it supplied by the taxpayers.

Soon after the Civil War, Americans in large numbers had middle-class incomes and the time and money to travel. It became fashionable to see Europe and, with the completion of the rail link to California, the wild and wooly western United States. Luxury liners set off on the seas, and luxury train lines were their landlocked counterparts. Thousands of Americans set out to see the country; they did it by rail, and if they had the money, they did it in high style.

OPPOSITE: A beautiful train on a beautiful stretch of railroad, SP No. 4449 runs southbound near Santa Barbara, California, during one of her occasional excursions out on the mainline.

ABOVE: This partially streamlined 4-6-4 (No. 1403) Hudson was built for passenger service on the New York, New Haven & Hartford.

The Overland Express

Union Pacific began promoting its service as soon as the rails were joined—fancy new Pullman sleeping cars for the rich, chair cars for the rest. Guidebooks like *Croftutt's New Overland Tourist* soon coached prospective sightseers on the risks and rewards of the adventure, and *Frank Leslie's Illustrated Weekly* sketched a somewhat different view.

First Class passage from New York to San Francisco was $136, and Second Class was $110. If you bought that First Class ticket, you were also entitled to book seats in one of the new sleeping cars, $14 additional for the Omaha to San Francisco portion of the trip. Second Class passengers had to make do with sleeping in their seats. It was, in the 1870s, guaranteed to be an eventful trip.

The locomotives were almost invariably sturdy, handsome American Standard 4-4-0 woodburners.

They were capable of running 40 or 50 miles per hour (64.36 or 80.45kph), but the crude roadbed of the transcontinental line made that very risky almost anywhere along the line. Instead, the Overland Express puttered along at 30 miles per hour (48.27kph) most of the time, and stopped frequently for water and fuel, and three times a day for meals. Average speed under the best conditions—assuming the trains were on time—was under 20 miles per hour (32.18kph).

The cars were lightweight, badly sprung, drafty, too cold or too hot, rattled and clattered incessantly, and were stuffed to the rafters with badly unwashed humanity—and that was the First Class cars. Survivors of the trip considered it luxurious, though, in comparison to the trials and tribulations of the pioneers who had crossed the plains and mountains afoot or in a Conestoga wagon. Soon the demand for tourist travel

became a foundation for some rail lines. Hotels and resorts blossomed all over the West, all catering to the travelers who would hop off the Overland Express, spend a day sightseeing and taking the waters, and then hop back on the Overland and off to something new.

Long-distance train travel inspired the railroads to provide a different kind of service than had been common previously, and sleeping cars made by Pullman, Wagner, and several other firms were attached to dining cars supplied and staffed for the production of excellent meals. The train became a landbound version of the luxury liner at sea, a comparison the railroads promoted—with all of the elegance, comfort, cuisine, and social relationships—but with better scenery and the chance to get off and walk around occasionally.

ABOVE: One of Union Pacific's handsome cars built for service on the Overland Limited. These wooden cars were the first and last word in luxury when put into service late in the nineteenth century, but would soon be superceded by heavyweight steel cars with many improvements.

OPPOSITE: While fast passenger trains got the publicity and the glory, fast freights made money for the railroads. This is one of the latter, an overland freight from the 1920s.

A RIDE ON THE OVERLAND EXPRESS

Luxury was as much in the eye of the beholder at the turn of the nineteenth century as it is at the turn of the twentieth. Here, Frank Leslie describes the ups and downs of a trip on the Overland Express in Frank Leslie's Illustrated Weekly, February 9, 1878:

From our Pullman hotel-car, the last in the long train, to the way-car which follows closely on the engine, there is a vast discount in the scale of comfort, embracing as many steps as there are conveyances. It is worth one's while to make a tour of the train for the sake of observing these differences and noting the manners and customs of traveling humanity, when tired bodies and annoyed brains (there are plenty of such even on the overland trip) have agreed to cast aside ceremony and social amenities and appear in easy undress.

The old assertion that man is at bottom a savage animal finds confirmation strong in a sleeping car, and as for the women—even with dear little five-and-three-quarter kids, the claws will come out upon these occasions. For here, at 9 PM, in the drawing-room sleeper, we find a cheerful musical party playing "Hold the Fort!" around the parlor organ, which forms its central decoration; three strong, healthy children running races up and down the aisle, and scourging each other with their parent's shawl straps; a consumptive invalid, bent double with a paroxysm of coughing; four parties, invisible but palpable to the touch, wrestling in the agonies of the toilet behind the closely but-toned curtains of their sections, and trampling on the toes of passers-by as they struggle with opposing draperies; a mother engaged in personal combat (also behind the curtains) with her child in the upper berth, and two young lovers, dead to all the world exchanging public endearments in a remote corner.

Who could bear these things with perfect equanimity? Who could accept with smiles the company of six adults at the combing and washing stages of ones' toilet? Who could rise in society, and under the close personal scrutiny of twenty-nine fellow-beings, jostle them in their seats all day, eat in their presence, take naps under their very eyes, lie down among them, and sleep—or try to sleep—within acute and agonized hearing of their faintest snores, without being ready to charge one's soul with twenty-nine distinct homicides?

But if the "drawing-room sleeper" be a place of trial to fastidious nerves, what is left to say of the ordinary passenger-car wherein the working-men and working-women . . . do congregate and are all packed like sardines in a box? It is a pathetic thing to see their nightly contrivances and poor shifts at comfort; the vain attempts to improvise out of their two or three feet [60.96 or 91.44cm] of space a comfortable sleeping place for some sick girl or feeble old person, and the weary, endless labor of the mothers to pacify or amuse their fretted children. Here and there some fortunate party of two or three will have full sway over a full section—two seats, that is to say—and there will be space for one of them to stretch his or her limbs in the horizontal posture and rest luxuriously; but, for the most part, every seat has its occupant, by night as well as by day, a congregation of aching spines and cramped limbs. The overland journey is no fairy tale to those who read it from a way car!

ABOVE: **The first Pullman sleepers were a bit more Spartan than they would later become. This is a good illustration of the type from around the 1870s or early 1880s, before the company added upholstery to the seats. These were the days of oil lamps and coal-burning stoves at the end of the car. Even so, this was the lap of luxury compared to the overnight accommodations in the chair cars.**

The Empire State Express

In some ways, the first of the real "classic" passenger trains was the New York Central's (NYC) legendary Empire State Express. Until the advent of the Empire State Express, railroad travel was a fairly slow, dreary business. You could cross the plains, but you did it at a sedate 25 or 35 miles per hour (40.23 or 56.32kph). Travel anywhere in the United States involved a lot of starting and stopping, and very little speed. That

changed when a passenger agent named George Henry Daniels (who would become an inspired and accomplished promoter) envisioned a high-speed, long-distance train offering premium transportation service to an upscale clientele.

A passenger agent couldn't implement an idea like this alone, and Daniels managed to catch the ear and imagination of the NYC's vice president, H. Walter

LEFT: New York Central & Hudson River Railroad's Empire State Express in its turn-of-the-century prime, a moment in history when only the best people rode this deluxe train—people who paid for the best, and got it.

ABOVE: Here's New York Central No. 870 and the Empire State Express, roaring down the track at about sixty miles per hour. That was the fastest scheduled passenger train in service at the time, 1893. At that rate, the Empire State Express made the run between Chicago and New York City in just twenty hours, far faster than any other passenger run of the time.

Webb. He pitched the idea of a fast train running between New York City on the east and Buffalo on the west, with brief stops at the state capital, Albany, and a few other select cities along the 439-mile route. After much planning and preparation, improved roadbed, a new, high-performance engine—and a lot of advance publicity, the NYC was ready to make a test run. Daniels proposed calling the new train the Empire State Express, and the idea was subsequently accepted.

That trial run departed New York City early on the morning of September 14, 1891, with the engine, tender, and five cars stuffed to the gills with newspapermen, and most of those stuffed with free champagne and dainty refreshments, compliments of the railroad. One of these cars was the "private varnish" of the NYC's vice president Webb, along to keep an eye on the proceedings and enjoy the excitement. The whole trip across New York state took just seven hours and six minutes; averaging better than 60 miles

per hour (96.54kph), including stops for coal and water.

A few weeks later, on October 26, the Empire State Express began scheduled revenue service, to rave reviews from the New York papers. *The Tribune's* editorial pages gushed the next day:

Seventy miles an hour was the time made for a part of the distance by the new express train (Empire State Express) on the New York Central Railroad in its run to Buffalo yesterday. The whole 440 miles (707.96 km) were covered in 8 hours and 40 minutes. The running of this train is a matter of universal interest since this is the fastest passenger service in the world. Naturally other railroads will be stimulated by the Central's experiment, and a general quickening of time by express trains may be looked for. That such a great speed can be made in safety and is to be a regular thing is a striking illustration of the progress made by the science of railroading.

LEFT: *New York Central's Empire State Express eastbound at Depew, New York,* behind a big Northern S1-b class 4-8-4, during a brisk December day in 1946, late in the train's illustrious life. This was a hopeful time for the railroads, a time when they were recovering from the hardships of war and before the airlines and highways sucked their customer base dry.

OPPOSITE: *Here's the Empire State Express* with typical heavyweight cars in the deepest, darkest days of the depression. At a time when all sorts of other institutions were collapsing and disappearing, when railroad employees around the nation were losing their jobs, the Empire State Express stayed on the rails, on an abbreviated schedule, and with the hopes of future prosperity. The locomotive is a J-1e Hudson, built in 1931.

NYC's Engine 999

George Henry Daniels' shrewd talent for publicity and free advertising got him a new and improved position, advertising manager for the railroad, and its first professional promoter. Part of his program to keep the NYC's name before the public in a favorable way was to set records whenever possible, and he would go to great lengths to accomplish this goal. In this case, that meant a special engine built to break speed records, the legendary No. 999.

Fabricated in the NYC's own shops, 999 was designed for speed, publicity, the Empire State Express, and headlines. On May 10, 1893, Engineer Charles Hogan coupled No. 999 to the cars of the train for the final part of the run to Buffalo, 150 miles (241.35km) to the west, and got his orders. He was asked to try to set a new speed record on the 36-mile (57.92km) straight section of right-of-way at the end of the run, after passing Batavia, New York, just before Buffalo.

After gliding through Batavia and getting his "high-ball" clearance for the block, Hogan pulled back the massive throttle bar until it was wide open. Mileposts went screaming past, the interval between each carefully measured by stopwatch. At one point, No. 999 and the Empire State Express rocketed down the rails at better than 112 miles per hour (180.21kph)—or, at least, that's what the cab crew claimed.

As expected, news of the accomplishment created a sensation. That was just what was intended, and Daniels and the NYC promotion department made sure everybody in the nation knew about it. The locomotive was pulled from revenue service and sent around the country on a publicity tour, ending up in Chicago, a place that would become "ground zero" for railroad publicity for many years to come.

No. 999's speed record lasted for many years and the engine itself is well-preserved today. Like so many other pretty faces, though, 999's days in the limelight were numbered. Within a few years another, newer locomotive had taken over the NYC's flagship passenger run, and by 1902, No. 999 was put out to pasture, hauling a slow milk train out in the western part of the state.

OPPOSITE: Certainly one of the most famous locomotives in American rail history, New York Central's No. 999 was specifically built for speed and to get media attention for the New York Central's Empire State Express running between New York and Chicago. Clocked unofficially at 112.5mph on one run, No. 999 created a sensation—and all the free publicity hoped for by the railroad. Here it is at an exposition in Chicago shortly after that record-setting 1893 run.

ABOVE: New York Central's legendary No. 999, freshly minted, poses for its baby picture on the day it was rolled out of the factory. This is a "builder's photograph," a routine document made by most locomotive manufacturers in the late nineteenth and early twentieth centuries. The photograph shows exactly what accessories and finishes were applied to the locomotive when delivered to the customer.

RIGHT: New York Central No. 999 in later life, with smaller drivers, still attracted a crowd in this shot from the 1920s during a run to South Bend, Indiana.

The New Empire State Express

In 1941, to celebrate fifty years, forty thousand runs, and seventeen million train-miles of accident-free operation, the NYC overhauled the Empire State Express with a complete makeover and new cars, and publicized the event with well-oiled newspaper reporters in the grand old tradition.

While other lines were converting to diesel as fast as they could, NYC commissioned ALCO to build massive, streamlined, and extremely powerful steam locomotives for the new trainsets. Covered by smooth stainless steel fairings, the new Hudsons looked like a bullet in flight and traveled nearly as fast.

The NYC had maintained a long love affair with the 4-6-4 Hudson design, buying and building hundreds of them since the first appeared in 1927. With cylinders 22 inches (55.88cm) across and a stroke of 29 inches (73.66cm), linked to driving wheels 6½ feet (1.98m) in diameter, these new J3a-class Hudsons were intended to be extremely fast. Each locomotive weighed 360,000 pounds (163,440kg), with a loaded tender (containing 14,000 gallons [53,200L] of water and thirty tons of coal) that was nearly as heavy.

The first of these special J3a Hudsons rolled out of the ALCO Schenectady plant four years earlier, in 1937, and would be followed by nine more. These agile engines provided nearly 4000hp at the drawbar, enough to easily move the sixteen cars of the new Empire State Express trainset down the road at high speed.

Two got stylish makeovers for the Empire State Express project, No. 5426 and No. 5429, with a streamlined fairing by the famed industrial designer Henry Dreyfuss, who developed the appearance and details of the whole train. The cars were built by Budd Manufacturing to match, and the whole package was extremely attractive. Budd used electric welding during the fabrication process, one of the reasons the cars were lighter, stronger, and quieter than the riveted steel designs of earlier years.

All the railroads of the time made a big point of the interior décor of their passenger trains, and NYC was no exception. Advertising materials promoting the 1941 introduction of the new Empire State Express crowed about the layout and furnishings, all designed by Paul Cret in conjunction with the NYC's engineering department. A brochure printed for the train's debut extolled the train's appointments:

Flourescent lighting, pleasing colors and unusual textures and finishes have been skillfully combined to produce an atmosphere of restful comfort, refinement and beauty. Air conditioning keeps cars at a comfortable temperature...

The new version of NYC's classic included two complete trainsets, one for each end of the line's daily runs. Included in each trainset were sixteen cars—a combination mail and baggage car following the tender, then another combination car, this one with a tavern and lounge plus more baggage stowage, then three parlor cars with deep armchairs, plus a dining car followed by four coaches, all followed up with an observation and buffet car. Each of the cars was 85 feet (25.91m) long, making the train span about a quarter mile in length (400m). And all of them used special rubber cushioning pads between the car body and the trucks to reduce vibration and noise.

All of the cars were plush and luxurious. The most elegant was the tavern-lounge-observation car at the back of the train. If you wanted to have a very good time all the way from New York to Detroit (the end of the line for the Empire State Express), the tavern car was the place to sit. Two card tables at the front of the car accommodated poker players of all abilities and a large semi-circular bar in the middle of the car provided high-test liquid refreshments for all tastes. More card tables were found in two booths on the left side, along with a row of comfortable sofas. Behind the bar, at the back of the car was the main lounge, with its semi-circular "solarium" offering

panoramic views of the passing countryside. A state-of-the-art radio provided entertainment for the passengers.

But you didn't need to limit yourself to the concoctions assembled at the back of the train; for variety, you could have a couple of highballs back there, stagger forward to the dining car and eat yourself silly on the extensive menu, all the while downing a few glasses of wine, perhaps followed by an after-dinner liqueur or two. Then, if you were still capable of mobility, you might want to crawl the rest of the way to the front of the train and the tavern car for another cocktail or two, just to see if the bartender there knew any special tricks with his liquid tranquilizers. After all this, you would probably want to have somebody toss your carcass in the baggage car, where you could pass out for the rest of the trip.

After all the time, trouble, imagination, talent, research, money, and publicity, the new and improved Empire State Express was set to kick off on a day that would sadly find all Americans deeply preoccupied with serious and somber concerns. The inauguration day was, unfortunately, December 7, 1941, the same day the Japanese bombed Pearl Harbor, pulling the United States into World War II. Luxurious train travel would be a thing of the past for the next few years.

Elegance on Wheels— The Pullman Story

For a full century, the name Pullman was synonymous with luxurious travel and elegance. At its peak, during the 1920s and '30s, millions of Americans slept in Pullman cars every year, 100,000 every night. George Pullman's empire was called "The Greatest Hotel on Earth."

Pullman wasn't the first to develop a railroad car set up to allow passengers to rest in comfort at night, but he perfected the sleeping car, and he effected a monopoly by swallowing up all the other operators of such cars.

Pullman's first cars were two modified coach cars built in 1859 at a cost of two thousand dollars each— just 44 feet (13.41m) long, with candles for light and a little stove for heat. They were put in service on the Chicago, Alton & St. Louis Railroad and had just three paying passengers on their inaugural run. Conductor

J. L. Barnes recalled much later that he had to ask the three to take their boots off before climbing into their new bunks. And when he complimented Pullman on the new car by observing that it was a fine car, Pullman replied, "It ought to be. It cost enough."

In 1865, Pullman developed a large, elegant, expensive sleeper, the *Pioneer*. It cost more than twenty thousand dollars, five times the cost of a normal chair car of the time, and was 58 feet (17.68m) long and more than 10 feet (3.05m) high. It was also wider than conventional cars—too wide for nearly every railroad. Then, President Lincoln was assassinated in April 1865, and the car was ordered attached to the funeral train. All down the line, carpenters quickly went to work modifying depot platforms and bridges, making room for the big car. After that, Pullman's sleepers were welcome across the nation.

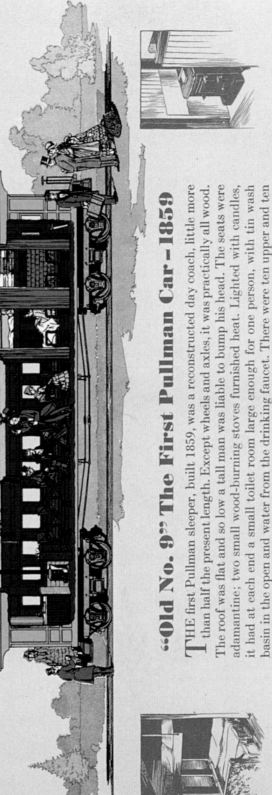

"Old No. 9" The First Pullman Car—1859

THE first Pullman sleeper, built 1859, was a reconstructed day coach, little more than half the present length. Except wheels and axles, it was practically all wood. The roof was flat and so low a tall man was liable to bump his head. The seats were adamantine; two small wood-burning stoves furnished heat. Lighted with candles, it had at each end a small toilet room large enough for one person, with tin wash basin in the open and water from the drinking faucet. There were ten upper and ten lower berths; mattresses and blankets, but no sheets. But it was the best yet.

OPPOSITE: Dinner is served, though nobody seems too thrilled in this photograph from about 1900. Dining car service could be a wonderful experience at that time, and Pullman and others put tremendous effort into making both the bill of fare and the surroundings excellent. This elaborate car has electric light, steam heat, and an attentive cast and crew.

ABOVE: Deluxe trains invariably included club cars like this one, where extra-fare and First Class passengers could spend their travel time chatting, reading, smoking, and drinking in absolute comfort. The styles of these lounges and their names changed a bit over the years, but the objective was always the same: complete luxury.

There was a lot of competition for passenger traffic after the Civil War, and after the completion of the transcontinental line in 1869, that competition became even more intense. The sleeping car business was just as competitive, and many companies built cars designed for overnight travel. Wagner, Rip Van Winkle, Gates, and the New York Central Sleeping Car Company were all struggling with Pullman for dominance after the Civil War.

Basically, each of these companies built cars with seats that could be folded flat, like a futon, and with upper berths that could be folded down. Early versions used flimsy fabric partitions between berths, with curtains facing the aisle. Later, more substantial partitions separated berths but the curtains stayed till the end—and were the source for endless stories and jokes about what happened when passengers climbed into berths to which they were not assigned.

Fairly early, Pullman, Wagner, and the others invested heavily in the interiors of these cars, making

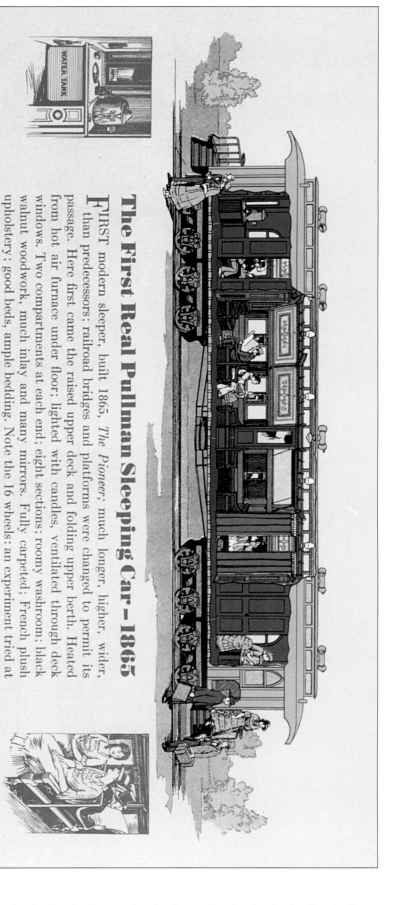

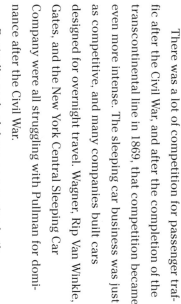

The First Real Pullman Sleeping Car – 1865

FIRST modern sleeper, built 1865, *The Pioneer;* much longer, higher, wider, than predecessors; railroad bridges and platforms were changed to permit its passage. Here first came the raised upper deck and folding upper berth. Heated from hot air furnace under floor; lighted with candles, ventilated through deck windows. Two compartments at each end; eight sections; roomy washroom; black walnut woodwork, much inlay and many mirrors. Fully carpeted; French plush upholstery; good beds, ample bedding. Note the 16 wheels; an experiment tried at this period but later abandoned in favor of 12, the present standard.

RIGHT: This is a typical heavyweight Pullman car of the 1930s and early '40s, the "Mounds." Pullman had developed mobile hospitality to a fine art about the time this car went into service, and the operation of this car and its kin would remain profitable for years to come.

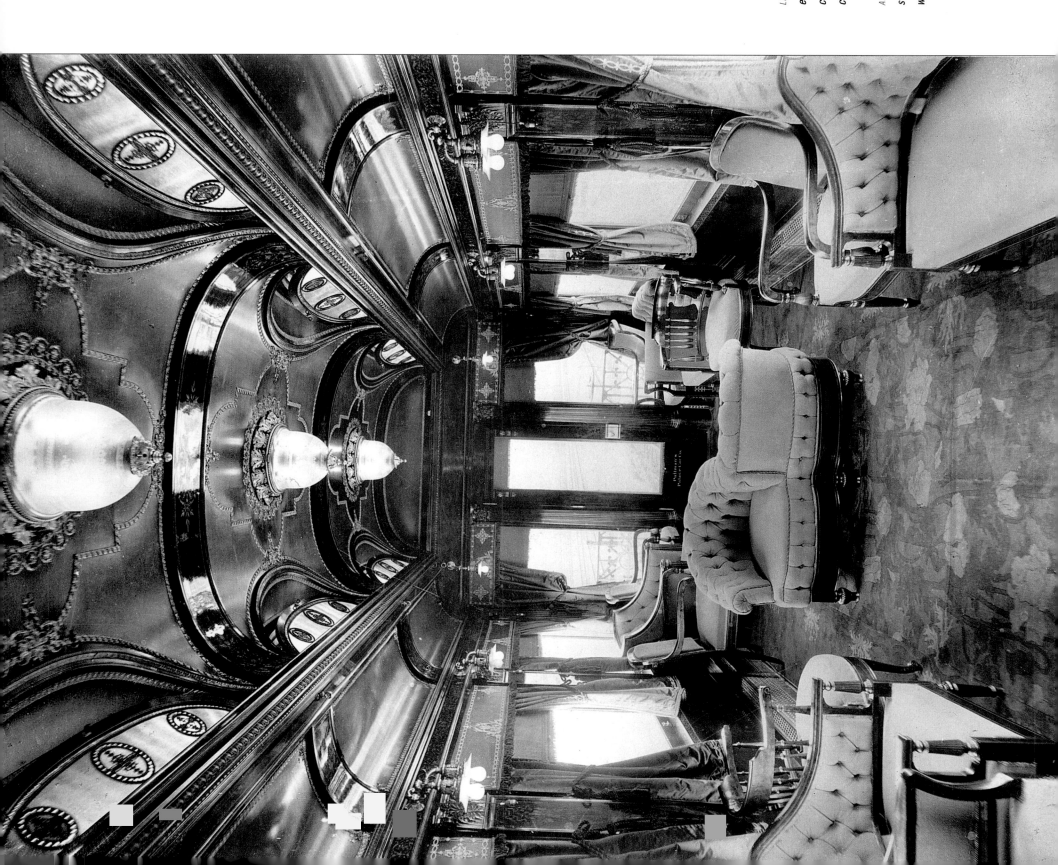

LEFT: *Pullman lounge cars like this one were not available to all passengers on early trains, but were reserved for the First Class and extra-fare clientele. Carefully constructed with veneer woods, large windows, and even with electric lights, these cars were designed for people accustomed to exclusive and deluxe comfort.*

ABOVE: *The introduction of the sleeping car created a lot of trauma for Victorian sensibilities. Bedding down with a large number of other human beings, male and female, with only a curtain for protection, was something of a radical notion in those days.*

The Steady March of Progress – 1876

CENTENNIAL year–1876–opened a period of further progress. The car's length grew from 58 to 70 feet. Oil lamps superseded candles. Air brakes appeared, making for greater speed and safety. A hot water heating system replaced stoves and furnaces. Six-wheel trucks were definitely adopted and overhead tanks with gravity supply system afforded water. Interior finish was in walnut, with carving, inlaying and lacquer work characteristic of the period.

The Car Vestibule Appears – 1887

THE car vestibule, marking an historical advance, appeared in 1887, strictly a Pullman invention. At first it merely enclosed a narrow passage between cars, to be widened later to full car width. It greatly enhanced comfort and safety. With twelve sections, drawing room, and smoking room, high backed seats, mahogany finish, much carving and ornamentation, higher windows, rich carpets and upholstery, and increasing elegance throughout, the Pullman was now blossoming into the full glory of the later Victorian period.

Comforts and Conveniences Multiply – 1891

THE wide vestibule is now in general use, with anti-telescoping construction. The car is growing longer–it is now 75 feet. Pintsch gas has become the standard illuminant, but electric lights are appearing, the result of long and painstaking experimentation. The car's exterior is of wood strip sheathing; ceilings of semi-empire design; and the air pressure water supply system has taken the place of hand pump and the gravity system previously employed.

LEFT: By the 1930s, Pullman diners had dispensed with the ornate interior décor and were offering legendary meals at bargain rates. The dining car seldom made money for the railroad, but the great food and give-away prices lured passengers aboard in droves.

ABOVE: The City of Los Angeles' club car, dubbed "The Little Nugget," was everything that a private club should be. Decked in rich wood veneers with ornate gilt trim, upholstered furniture, and even a canary in a cage, this was the spot for brandy and cigars after dinner.

them as close to an elegant, upscale residence or private club as possible—and charging extra for the service.

And these sleeping car builders didn't just manufacture the cars, but owned and operated them, splitting the proceeds with the railroads on whose rails the cars traveled. It was a great service, and a great deal for everybody.

Service on these premium cars evolved into something memorable. Pullman porters were renowned for their graceful manners, skilled ability to serve the most demanding customer, and handsome appearance—and no wonder, because Pullman trained and supervised them carefully. The simple act of serving a bottle of beer involved twelve precise steps, each of which the porter had to memorize and perform flawlessly.

In time, Pullman cars would offer greater privacy—drawing rooms and roomettes, all-room cars, then private showers and toilets in each room instead of at the end of the car. Pullman developed,

refined, and operated club and dining cars, stocked them with the best provisions and liquid refreshments, and staffed them with barmen, cooks, waiters, and stewards of such sterling qualities that they became legendary.

At its peak, the Pullman organization employed many thousands of people to manufacture its cars, service them, launder the sheets and table-cloths, print the menus and training manuals, and keep them clean and tidy.

The crash in passenger rail traffic after World War II severely reduced Pullman's profits. The company was liquidated on January 3, 1968, slightly more than a century after it had been founded with those two primitive little cars and such high hopes.

ABOVE: *Lightweight stainless steel construction replaced heavy steel cars after World War II, and Pullman had a name for each one; this is the City of Saint Louis. When this photograph was taken, about 1950, passenger traffic was already in deep decline; the attendant may be wondering where everybody went.*

LEFT: *The Spirit of Saint Louis was a deluxe, all-Pullman sleeper train operated by Pennsylvania Railroad. It is seen here headed into the yard a few months before American involvement in World War II began. After December 7, 1941, rail service would be transformed, and the days of comfort and ease would be replaced by standing room only, passengers sitting on their bags in the aisles.*

OPPOSITE: *In the days when it was still legal to smoke on commercial transportation, passengers on deluxe trains repaired to elegant club cars like the Chicago, Burlington & Quincy's "Omaha Club" solarium lounge. Here, with massive stogies, pipes, and cigarettes, they would gossip, flirt, and visit, watching the miles roll past and waiting for the server to come through with another tray of martinis.*

The All-Steel Car Appears—1907

No other advance in car building made so much for safety as all-steel construction. Following the first experimental steel car, in 1907, the type was adopted in general service in 1910. Length 74 feet; full vestibule; 12 sections, drawing room and smoking room; steel sheathed outside; electric light from axle device; low pressure vapor heat system. Interiors were by this time becoming more quiet, moderate and tasteful, with plain, mottled finish, green frieze plush upholstery and green carpets. This was the period of standardization.

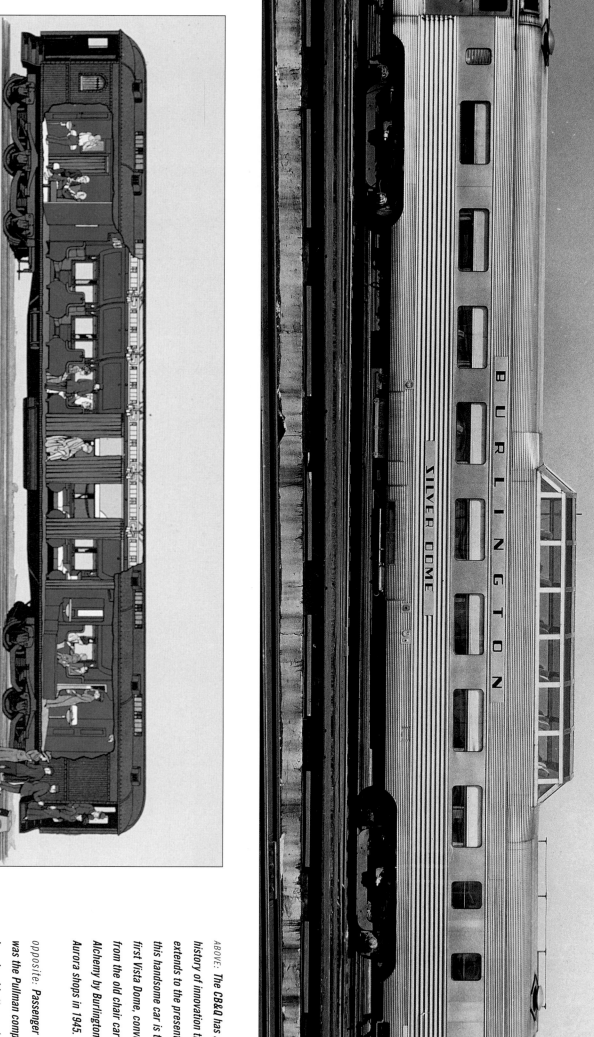

ABOVE: The CB&Q has a long history of innovation that extends to the present, but this handsome car is the very first Vista Dome, converted from the old chair car Silver Alchemy by Burlington's Aurora shops in 1945.

OPPOSITE: Passenger travel was the Pullman company's bread and butter, and their advertising never failed to remind folks that when it came to traveling by rail, comfort was synonymous with Pullman.

Refinements and Conveniences – 1920

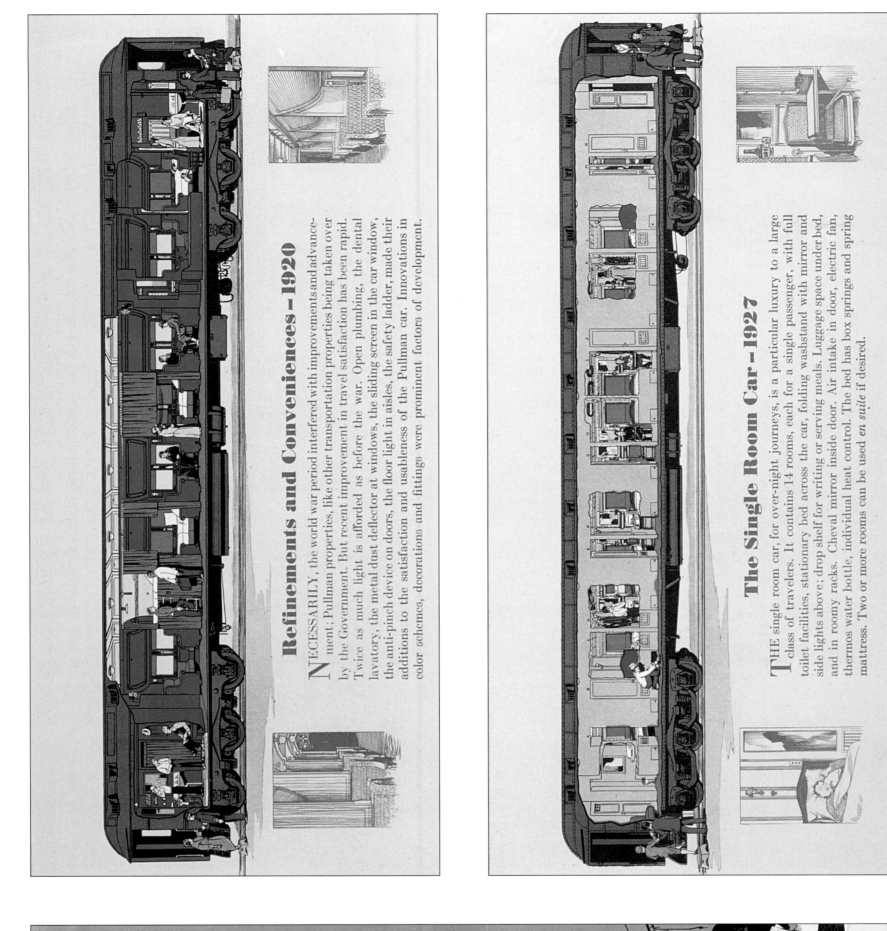

NECESSARILY, the world war period interfered with improvements and advancement; Pullman properties, like other transportation properties being taken over by the Government. But recent improvement in travel satisfaction has been rapid. Twice as much light is afforded as before the war. Open plumbing, the dental lavatory, the metal dust deflector at windows, the sliding screen in the car window, the anti-pinch device on doors, the floor light in aisles, the safety ladder, made their additions to the satisfaction and usableness of the Pullman car. Innovations in color schemes, decorations and fittings were prominent factors of development.

The Single Room Car – 1927

THE single room car, for over-night journeys, is a particular luxury to a large class of travelers. It contains 14 rooms, each for a single passenger, with full toilet facilities, stationary bed across the car, folding washstand with mirror and side lights above; drop shelf for writing or serving meals. Luggage space under bed, and in roomy racks. Cheval mirror inside door. Air intake in door, electric fan, thermos water bottle, individual heat control. The bed has box springs and spring mattress. Two or more rooms can be used *en suite* if desired.

9 ways to travel in comfort

by PULLMAN

THE GRAND CENTRAL TERMINALS

In the early days of rail travel, passengers usually traveled from big city to big city, and the final destination was always a major city. At the end of the line, passengers debarked at the final depot, known as a terminal. Since each railroad line had its own specific terminal within the city limits, travelers who needed to transfer from train to train were required to take a trip across town to another terminal. The transfers from train to train could prove to be quite a cumbersome task.

Commodore William H. Vanderbilt changed depot history when he decided to build a single terminal to serve all of his railroad lines. New York City's Grand Central Terminal was built in 1871 to accommodate Vanderbilt's New York Central & Hudson River Railroad, the New York & Harlem Railroad, and the New York, New Haven & Hartford Railroad. It was an impressive building, one that promoted all of the Vanderbilt lines and proved to be a tremendous convenience to passengers.

Noting the success of the Grand Central Terminal in New York, other cities that aspired to this level of urban tact found ways to build their own "grand" terminals. Between 1872 and 1892, about twenty cities followed suit and built large terminals that served more than one rail line. In some cases, the terminals were financed cooperatively by the railroads served, and in other cases, the station was built by the local government. Regardless of how the grand terminals were financed, the reasons behind them were simple and similar: establishing a "Grand Central Terminal" marked a city as a major metropolitan destination worthy of cosmopolitan travelers.

But the establishment of these terminals proved to offer other benefits to the local municipality. Locomotives are noisy, dirty, and dangerous engines that spew soot and ash all along their paths. Consolidating various railroad lines to meet in a single terminal not only reduced pollution and hazards, but also provided opportunity for a lucrative service industry to grow. Amenities such as coffee shops, refreshment kiosks, and other shops catering to waiting passengers were established within the terminal.

LEFT AND BELOW: Penn Station opened in 1910 and was a monument that rivaled great European structures. The architect, Charles McKim, had been influenced by Roman architecture, especially the famous baths. Now only a memory, the destruction of the magnificent Penn Station galvanized thousands of citizens into action, demanding laws to protect America's architectural gems.

By the turn of the ninteenth century, with the advent of popular electrical use for motive power, the concept of the "grand terminal" needed to be re-defined, as major cities outgrew their grand terminals. A new wave of building larger and grander terminals began in the heart of New York City, this time with the construction of New York's Pennsylvania Station. The construction of New York's Pennsylvania Station challenged Vanderbilt's stronghold on New York and escalated the rivalry between the Vanderbilt lines and the Pennsylvania Railroad.

The Pennsylvania Railroad buried their railroad lines underground by tunneling under the East River and the Hudson River. Removing the noise, dirt, and odor of railroad traffic had the effect of projecting a high-class atmosphere. Their new grand terminal was modeled after a Roman temple and imitated the ancient Baths of Caracalla. Opened in 1910, the Pennsylvania Station set new standards for depot design.

Not to be outdone, Vanderbilt's Grand Central Station would also be overhauled; construction for the two competing terminals happened simultaneously. In addition to streamlined conveniences, the new Grand Central Station would also be served by electric railways that allowed passengers to transfer to New York's subways. Vanderbilt's new terminal opened in 1913 and was known as the "Terminal City," with three thousand people working in its shops and thirty thousand passengers passing through its halls each day.

For the next fifteen years, cities with the economic resources either rebuilt or replaced their aging terminals. However, this renaissance came to an end in 1929 with the onset of the Great Depression. In the years since, many of the grand terminal buildings have been demolished, but a few stunning examples live on as architectural treasures. The Saint Louis Union Station (1894) and the Indianapolis Union Station (1889) are two outstanding stations which survive from the first wave of terminal construction.

There are also a handful of notable Grand Central Stations from the second wave of terminal building that have survived. New York's Grand Central Station—beautifully restored in the 1990s and still serving passengers—remains the grandest of all. Kansas City's magnificent Union Station, the third largest terminal in America when it opened in 1914, is now a museum. And Cincinnati's beautiful Moderne-style station was probably the last and most expensive terminal, costing over twenty million hard-to-come-by Depression dollars when it opened in 1933. These architectural feats remain true to their intended purpose and still hold the trappings of development for the cities that host them.

ABOVE: New York's Grand Central Terminal lives up to its name. A "City within the City," it covered over 30 city blocks and boasted that it could handle a thousand trains a day.

RIGHT: New York visitors and commuters alike can still experience this spectacular moment from the Golden Age of railroad building. Grand Central Terminal is just one of the small handful of grand terminals that have survived.

The Best That Money Could Buy—New York Central's Twentieth Century Limited

America and Americans have changed so much since the Twentieth Century Limited was in its prime during the 1940s and '50s that it is almost as difficult a phenomenon to appreciate as the Crusades or the French Revolution. It was a time when America had a royal class, and our royalty rode the rails. And the railroad of choice was the New York Central, especially the Twentieth Century Limited (or its near duplicate and long-time rival, the Broadway Limited). For fifty years and more, this marvelous, five-star landbound version of a luxury liner carried the rich and famous and elite between Chicago's LaSalle Street Station and New York's Grand Central, usually in about eighteen hours, and always in the best possible style.

It seems difficult to believe now, but before the age of private jets, movie stars, best-selling authors, corporate presidents, and every other member of the priveleged class traveled in what were essentially

their own private rail cars—"private varnish" in the trade vernacular—but most liked to see and be seen among others of their class, and railroads catered to them aggressively. Santa Fe's Super Chief was the only acceptable train for the upper crust of the film industry traveling between Chicago and Los Angeles, for example. And if they were traveling on to New York (and most were), the only real acceptable choices were equally deluxe trains, the Broadway Limited or the Twentieth Century Limited. Both traversed the distance (980 mostly flat miles [1,576.82km] for the Century, 902 partly mountainous miles [1,451.32km] for the Broadway) on the same schedule, at the same time, almost from their inception at the very beginning of the twentieth century.

Both the Broadway Limited and the Twentieth Century Limited had their genesis in the great World's

Columbian Exposition of 1893, held in Chicago to celebrate American technology and progress of all kinds. Railroads were a big part of the exposition, and both the major and minor companies in the railroad industry did everything possible to attract attention and recruit both passenger and freight traffic to their lair.

New York Central (NYC) and Pennsylvania Central were the biggest, baddest boys on the block at that time, and both determined to provide passenger service between New York and Chicago during the exposition at unheard-of speeds. NYC's was the Exposition Flyer, running on an amazing twenty-hour schedule, and Penn Central's version, called the Pennsylvania Special, moved almost as fast. The Flyer was grounded after the fair, but the Special evolved into the Broadway Limited.

Running a passenger train at very high speeds is difficult enough on an occasional basis or for a short time, but doing it routinely is another matter. It takes tremendous coordination and preparation—of the very rails and roadbed, of the locomotives and equipment, and of the whole complex schedule of routine traffic using the same right of way. All railroads of the time offered "crack" or express passenger trains, and they seemed fast enough at the time—averaging 40 or 45 miles (64.36 or 72.41km) an hour, perhaps, and complete with Pullman sleeping cars and curtained berths.

NYC had upgraded their fleet during the 1890s and replaced lighter rail with massive 100-pound-per-yard tracks (45.4kg per 91.44cm) for durability, a smoother ride, and higher speeds. By 1902, NYC was ready to compete with the Penn Central for the "carriage trade," and they did it with a train originally called the Twentieth Century. The name was adjusted almost immediately to make the comparison with Penn Central's express, now christened the Broadway

LEFT: In its heyday, the Twentieth Century Limited had multiple "sections," or duplicate trains, ready to handle the passenger traffic between the principal cities of the United States. One of the joys of such travel was sitting on the platform of a parlor observation car like this "Valley" type built by Pullman, watching the world go by.

ABOVE: A vintage ad announces new service on board the Burlington Route and other lines.

OPPOSITE: New York Central No. 5271 is a powerful ALCO Hudson, one of 145 similar J-1a-e engines built between 1927 and 1931, with the Twentieth Century Limited in tow. The 4-6-4 Hudson was a popular locomotive for fast passenger trains like this one.

Limited, unavoidable; it was thereafter known as the Twentieth Century Limited.

When it was first advertised, the NYC declared that the new train would maintain a twenty-hour schedule between the two cities. At the time, this was roughly equivalent to offering supersonic service; it was impossibly fast in the experience of almost anybody, and was declared impossible in both the popular and industry press. Nonetheless, on June 15, 1902, the Twentieth Century Limited began revenue service, departing Grand Central Station at a quarter to three in the afternoon, just in time for a whiskey sour or two. That was followed by a long, luxurious dinner, a restful sleep, breakfast, and a stately arrival at Chicago's Grand Central Station at quarter till ten the next day. "Nine hundred eighty miles in just twenty hours.—It Saves A Day!" proclaimed the advertisements.

In command of the locomotive No. 4695, a glittering 2-6-2 Prairie-class, was one of the NYC's most trusted engineers, Thomas Sherwood, with Thomas Jordan doing the honors with the shovel over on the

right side of the cab.

Back in the dining or the club car was the legendary and eccentric John "Bet-A-Million" Gates, a very wealthy and somewhat uncouth industrialist who came along just for the ride. Gates, never at a loss for words, was asked by reporters how he liked the trip. His comment was that the Twentieth Century Limited would surely make New York a suburb of Chicago—just the sort of quote beloved by newspapermen and railroad publicists both. Gates enjoyed the trip so much that he hopped back aboard for the return run, and when the reporters in New York asked him about the experience he said, "The Twentieth Century Limited is destined to make Chicago a suburb of New York!" He was, in fact, right both times.

The consist on that inaugural day was assembled from extremely elegant Wagner parlor and sleeper cars, as it would be for years. And for years it would have a diner and club car serving food and drink of stellar quality and at prices well above those on other trains. Dinner, for example, was $1.50 at a time when other trains would feed you five or six substantial courses

LEFT: Cloaked in industrial designer Henry Dreyfuss' groundbreaking streamlined sheath, the Twentieth Century Limited quickly became the most recognizable train in the United States.

ABOVE: After making the 900-mile (1,448.1km) trip from New York to Chicago in a mere twenty hours, the Twentieth Century was dubbed the train that would "make New York a suburb of Chicago," and vice-versa.

OPPOSITE: The Twentieth Century Limited was a highly successful premium train when the New York Central restyled its power with streamlined J-3a class Hudson locomotives.

for a single dollar. But the Twentieth Century Limited's dinner was sumptuous far beyond the normal meal, just one of the details of the operation that got the attention of the traveling public and railroad publicity men of the day. Those Wagner diners were paneled in rich, dark woods, heavily ornamented and illuminated by ornate leaded-glass windows and transoms overhead. Before and after dinner, patrons retired to the lounge and observation car *Euxodus* at the end of the train for a drink—both the drink and its twenty-five-cent price were quite stiff by the standards of the day.

The whole marketing idea behind the Twentieth Century Limited was to appeal not to the common traveler but to the most elegant and select of American society. The speed of the train helped with that. So did the lavish services aboard. But the thing that really filtered out the unwashed multitude was an extra fare for passage—eight dollars over and above the normal tariff for passage between New York and Chicago in 1902, a very substantial sum for all but the most well-to-do.

The Twentieth Century Limited was an extremely popular train right from the very beginning. Demand for accommodation was so strong that the NYC almost always added one or more "extras." An extra is essentially a duplicate train, complete in every detail, following the first train five or ten minutes down the track. In the case of the Twentieth Century Limited, that meant two or three or up to seven complete Twentieth Century Limiteds departing for Chicago or New York on any given day. Each of these trains had the same standard of service and the same grade of excellent barbers, cooks, dining car stewards, and maids. Each had cars of the same superb quality, and drinks in the bars at the head or end of the train of the same potency. The cut flowers in the private rooms and public lounges were just as fresh and just as costly. To the upper class of that time, the surcharge was well worth the improved service.

All that dark paneling disappeared with a radical makeover in 1938. Henry Dreyfuss, one of America's leading industrial designers, completely restyled the

Twentieth Century Limited in a fashion we would today call "moderne." Gone was the brass-mounted vestibule, replaced by an enclosed and elegant solarium. The dark wood and old-fashioned chairs disappeared and bright, sleek, smooth versions appeared in their stead.

But the most impressive part of the new Twentieth Century Limited, and the thing that is considered today Dreyfuss' masterpiece was his external treatment of the train's power. NYC bought heavy, very fast Hudson locomotives for their flagship passenger run, and Dreyfuss customized them with a very distinctive streamlined shroud. The result was a locomotive that was easily recognized by anybody—in a newsreel, on the pages of *Life*, or in its living personification, blasting down the tracks. There was nothing like it anywhere.

Throughout its long life, the Twentieth Century Limited was the preferred choice of the rich and famous—Theodore Roosevelt, Booth Tarkington, Lillian Russell, J. P. Morgan, Gloria Swanson, Spencer Tracy, Ginger Rogers, and almost anyone else of particular note. If you had the money for it, and the

clothes, and the manners, you would find yourself rubbing elbows with such people in the lounge after dinner, a place that was full of good conversation, cigarette smoke, laughter, wit, and wisdom.

Somehow or other, the Twentieth Century Limited lasted all the way into the 1960s. Of course, those incredible Hudsons finally wore out and were replaced by diesels. And the whole notion of scheduled deluxe passenger rail service was worn out as well. After six and a half decades of legendary service, the Twentieth Century Limited made its last run in 1967.

OPPOSITE: The Twentieth Century Limited was restyled and presented to the press on September 9, 1948, halted here for a photographic portrait of the whole new train. Gone were the old heavyweight cars, replaced by lightweight streamlined versions.

ABOVE LEFT AND RIGHT: Travel via the "water level route" on board any of the New York Central's stunning streamliners promised spectacular sights by day and quiet and comfort by night, as these vintage 1950s advertisements attest.

LEFT: This ALCO sales card features the complete specifications for the Hudson locomotives built for the New York Central's famous streamliners.

One by one, the windows close their eyes

. . . for a wonderful Water Level Route sleep

Nighttime on New York Central. Long ago, the last, leisurely dining car patron pushed back his chair with a contented sigh.

Only a few night owls still chat over refreshments in the club car. One by one, shades come down and lights go out as this great hotel-on-wheels glides along gentle, low-level valleys. The guests, in their Pullman private rooms, drift off to slumberland . . . with a downy comfort and a deep-down sense of all-weather security no skyway or highway can match.

GOING OUR WAY? Throughout this area, you'll find New York Central streamliners and dreamliners to make your trips a daylight delight or an overnight vacation.

New York Central

The Water Level Route—You Can Sleep

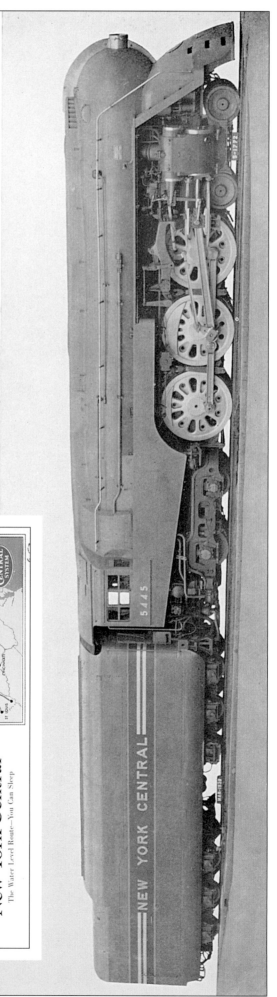

New York Central Hudson streamlined for Twentieth Century Limited	
Road numbers of this series	5445-5454
Built	Alco, 1938
Cylinders, diameter and stroke, in.	22½ x 29
Diameter of drivers, in.	79
Tractive force, lbs. engine, 43,400; booster, 12,100	
Boiler pressure, lbs. per sq. in.	275
Total weight of engine, lbs.	365,500
Weight on drivers, lbs.	201,800
Weight on leading truck, lbs.	67,100
Weight on trailing truck, lbs.	96,600
Weight of engine and tender, lbs.	681,800
Grate area, sq. ft.	82
Evaporative heating surface, sq. ft.	4187
Superheater heating surface, sq. ft.	1745
Tender capacity: Tons of coal	28
Gallons of water	13,600

NEW YORK CENTRAL

5445

HENREY DREYFUSS' TWENTIETH CENTURY LIMITED

Young Henry Dreyfuss had worked in theater design under the then-famous Norman Bel Geddes during the early 1930s, then struck out on his own, styling all sorts of consumer and industrial products. His approach was to keep in mind the ultimate utility of the product. Instead of the conventional term "streamlined," he preferred to call his treatment "cleanlined" instead.

The signature piece of any train is its locomotive, and the NYC made sure that the power on the point for the Twentieth Century Limited would get the attention of the press and the public. Henry Dreyfuss took an essentially standard (but state of the art) Hudson-class 4-6-4 locomotive and added a shroud to cut wind resistance at speed—and to make the locomotive look like it was at speed even when standing still.

The basic design of the engines used on the Twentieth Century Limited was introduced in 1927 and came to full flower with Dreyfuss' 1938 version, the J-3a. Ten of these were built by ALCO with the full Dreyfuss treatment. Huge 79-inch (200.66cm) drivers, finished with aluminum paint, immediately caught the eye of any beholder. The smooth skirt and tender were painted light gray, with a trip stripe of dark gray and blue to match on the cars.

The whole train was styled, right down to the silver in the dining cars, the menus, and even the matchbook covers. His treatment inside and out was understated grace and elegance, with clean, smooth surfaces and corners, unostentatious, and very comfortable. For a generation that was used to more potted palms that you'd find in an upscale Victorian-era French whorehouse, the effect was refreshing beyond belief.

OPPOSITE: *Dreyfuss' streamlined design for the Twentieth Century Limited quickly became a railroad icon. This charming poster features the famed locomotive.*

ABOVE: *Here comes the Twentieth Century Limited at speed, roaring past Oscawana, New York, in July 1938. The external treatment was done by famed designer Henry Dreyfuss in what is now called "Art Deco" style. Although the streamlining didn't really help cut wind resistance very much, it certainly made the train instantly recognizable and distinct from the competition.*

Broadway Limited

While many of the 1930s rich and famous considered the Twentieth Century Limited the very last word in elegance, an approximately equal number of the select chose Pennsylvania Railroad's Broadway Limited. The two trains existed in parallel universes—both equally fast, both fitted with Pullman sleepers, both styled by celebrity designers, and both offering five-star food and drink service.

This premier service began way back in 1887 with a deluxe service called the Pennsylvania Limited. Configured without a single chair car and exclusively assembled from Pullman sleepers, this original New York to Chicago train was intended to filter out the riffraff with high tariffs, and generally succeeded in doing so. These new cars were all equipped with full vestibules, an innovation at the time. These vestibules linked and enclosed the ends of adjoining cars, making passage down the length of the train safe and comfortable. Vestibules also provided a kind of shock-absorber function that cushioned the movement of the cars during acceleration and braking, formerly a major discomfort.

This Pennsylvania Limited was a small consist, just a composite baggage and sleeper car, a diner, and three full Pullmans, with another sleeper tied on between Cincinnati and New York. All of these cars were glossy and ornamented in the best tradition of the high-Victorian age—gleaming dark green paint and glass on the outside, ornate carved wood and brocade inside. Prices were steep in the diner—porterhouse steak was seventy-five cents, an omelet spiked with rum cost forty cents. Any café alongside the tracks would provide the same dishes for fifteen cents or less—but without the cachet of this new deluxe form of transportation.

Then, the following year, the Pennsy commissioned a whole new set of cars for the Limited. Brewster Green continued to be the base color for the cars, but now the window line was finished in a

bright, light yellow, with red above that in the letterboard area. This paint scheme made the Limited easily identifiable, and it was soon called "the Yellow Kid" by passengers, railroad workers, and everybody along the right-of-way.

These cars were even more ornate inside. One car even included a bridal suite, and polished veneers of rare and beautiful woods were standard. Usual for this age were the electric lights, one of the novel features of diners on the run. Included were a parlor car with smoking lounge and library, a dining car, and three Pullman sleepers, all followed up by the last car with its lavish compartments and observation platform.

As grand as this was, the fame of this operation didn't really begin until 1902 and the beginning of an

eighteen-hour schedule between Chicago and New York. At the time, the best passenger trains were taking twenty-eight hours to cover the distance; the Pennsy proposed to do it in twenty in newspaper ads appearing on June 8. The first run was on the eleventh, and on the fifteenth, the New York Central began the same service on the same schedule, departing at the same time. It was the start of a great race that captured the attention of the nation, most of which was far too poor to ever ride in either train.

Of course, that first run had newspapermen and Pennsy executives as its primary cargo, and the free ride for the journalists (and free drinks and dinners) paid off nicely the next day. The papers were awash in reports about the enthusiastic crowds who lined the

ABOVE: From its inception, the Broadway Limited was considered a premium train, designed for passengers of taste and discernment.

OPPOSITE: The Broadway Limited, like the Twentieth Century Limited, was often sold out. The result was the addition of duplicate trains running one after the other, each known as a section. These gentlemen are waiting to take the tickets of the first and second sections on the anniversary of the inaugural run.

rails to watch, cheer, and wave as the Pennsylvania Special shot past. And it really did make good time—127 miles per hour (214.34kph) for one three-mile (4.83km) stretch, if the stopwatches of the crew can be believed.

The great competition with the Twentieth Century Limited began on Sunday, June 15, 1902, and actually benefited both trains. When both westbound trains were on time, they traveled on parallel tracks for several miles before entering Chicago. Passengers enjoyed the appearance of a race, although the railroads both strictly prohibited such competitions, and cheered when their train pulled ahead.

Just as with the Twentieth Century Limited, the quality of the food and drink on the Pennsylvania Limited was superb. A $1.50 dinner was one of the major attractions, but the tranquilizers served in the bar car, and the witty, charming conversation that went with them, brought other accomplished people aboard.

Pennsy changed the name of the train to the Broadway Limited in 1925, and maintained its status as the flagship passenger train of the company. That

status was further enhanced in a decision that made the train immortal—the re-styling of the whole operation with new cars, new power, and a new look. The Pennsylvania Railroad brought in famous industrial designer Raymond Loewy and architect Paul Cret to create a new image for its best passenger trains, and it called the result the "Fleet of Modernism—The Blue Ribbon Trains."

The Broadway Limited retained its luxurious foundation with an all-Pullman consist, complete with individual showers in passengers' rooms (which was a first). The whole train was restricted to private rooms only, without a single upper berth anywhere.

Travel time continued to drop over the years, down to sixteen hours westbound, and fifteen and a half hours to New York in the 1960s. The Broadway Limited lasted longer than almost any other prestige train, longer than its old rival the Twentieth Century Limited, winning the race for longevity. Even at the end, the Broadway Limited retained its standards for excellence while other passenger operations were becoming shopworn and ragged.

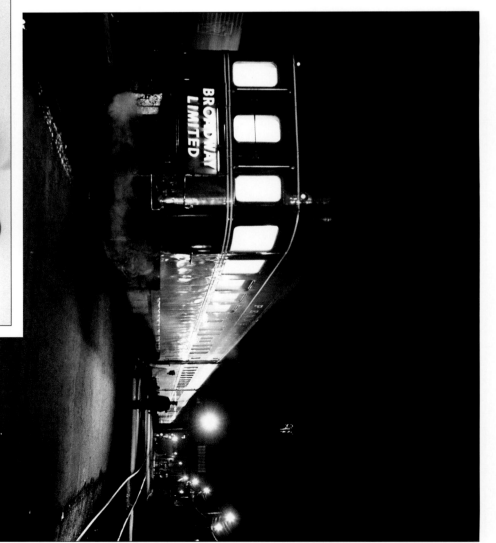

ABOVE: The end of the line for the Broadway Limited came on the night this photograph was made with the last run of this all-Pullman sleeper train running between New York and Chicago.

LEFT: The Pennsylvania Railroad's Broadway Limited under tow by a stalwart K-4 in September, 1935.

RAYMOND LOEWY'S BROADWAY LIMITED

The public's attention was engaged by the New York Central's Twentieth Century Limited, but the Pennsylvania Railroad's competing train was styled by just as daring and famous an industrial designer as Henry Dreyfuss, the older, charismatic Raymond Loewy. Born in France, Loewy had a highly theatrical personal style that helped make his name a household word during the 1930s, and helped attract many clients like the Pennsylvania Railroad.

Loewy's first railroad client was the Pennsylvania Railroad and his first locomotive was the huge, quarter-million Depression-era dollars pure electric GG-1 in 1934. This monster was essentially two 4-6-0 ten-wheel locomotives grafted back to back. Without all the steam running gear, Loewy was able to give the exterior of the GG-1 smooth, aerodynamic lines unlike the cluttered, boxy appearance of traditional electrics. To this, he and his team (which included people from the Pennsylvania railroad, Westinghouse, General Electric, Baldwin, and Gibbs & Hill, consulting engineers) added a rich, dark green paint and five gold pinstripes running the whole length of the locomotive and "Pennsylvania" in clean, sparse, san-serif lettering.

But Loewy's treatment of the Broadway Limited and its S-1 locomotive really got the attention of the American public. The first of these was based on a K4 variant of the Pacific 4-6-2 locomotive, Pennsylvania Railroad's No. 3768. This was an older locomotive when it was brought into the shops, having entered service in 1920. But the rebuild was a thorough one, more than just skin deep.

The skin, though, was where Loewy's talents were directed. He and the Pennsylvania Railroad engineering department made wind tunnel tests to determine the

proper basic shape for the streamlined shroud. They came up with something that rather closely resembled the competition, with a profile that was almost identical to Dreyfuss' J-3a Hudson. But Loewy's Pacific was almost completely enclosed in its shroud, right down to the running gear and drivers. It, too, was adorned with gray paint, although of a darker hue, and with elegant gold pinstripes and lettering.

The Broadway Limited was very similar to the Twentieth Century Limited in every way, and certainly had its own devotees and admirers. Its club and lounge cars were spacious, elegant, and stylish. A beautiful quarter-circle bar kept the patrons just as lubricated and tranquil as the ones on the Century. But there were enough variations that travelers—at least those wealthy enough to have experienced both—typically preferred one to the other. And all of them seemed happy with their choices.

ABOVE: *Designer Raymond Loewy strikes a pose with one of his signature designs. The two trains are Pennsylvania Railroad K4 Pacifics, before and after Loewy's treatments.*

LUCIUS BEEBE AND THE TWENTIETH CENTURY LIMITED

Railroading, particularly passenger railroading of the deluxe kind, had no more impassioned advocate than Lucius Beebe, for many years one of America's most brash and outspoken columnists. After a long career as the best-dressed cub reporter on The New York Herald, Beebe wrote steam-powered prose for Gourmet magazine, The New Yorker, and Town & Country magazine, and was a columnist for the San Francisco Examiner.

An unapologetic elitist, it was Beebe's basic premise that any person worth knowing should have had the good sense to be born to parents with lots of money, most of it old, and should possess excellent social standing, plus personal talent, wit, and charm. He loathed airplanes, automobiles (except the better classes of Rolls-Royces), and most people.

Beebe celebrated trains of all kinds after World War II, but especially the Twentieth Century Limited, which he featured in many articles and books. He loved train travel so much that he was co-owner of a private railroad car of elegant and costly dimensions, and used it from time to time to deplete his large personal fortune.

Beebe's notion of heaven appears to have been a place where God wears bib overalls and sits on a throne facing forward in the cab of a gleaming Hudson-class steam locomotive, a place where the apostles all work for the New York Central, and where the lesser angels can be found reliably waiting at the elbow of the good and the just with a magnum of superb French champagne and a tray of crackers and Beluga caviar.

RIGHT: Bon vivant and dandy Lucius Beebe was a railroad enthusiast and a Twentieth Century Limited loyalist. The columnist, whose credits included Gourmet magazine, found the menu on board the New York Central's star train sufficiently elegant to suit his refined palate.

DINING SERVICE
NEW YORK CENTRAL LINES

HORS D'OEUVRES—Green Olives 25   Hearts of Celery 35   Sliced Tomatoes 45   India Relish 20
Ripe Olives 25   Melon Mangoes 25   Midget Ghetrini 25
French Sardines in Olive Oil 75

Our Specialties

BISQUE OF NEW TOMATOES AND PEAS, Cup.....30   Tureen.....45   EGGS ON HEARTS OF LETTUCE, Tartare Sauce.....85

CONSOMME, HOT.....Cup 25;   Jellied Cup 40   NEW POTATOES IN CREAM.....40

CLAM BROTH.....(Cup) 30   VELOUTE OF NEW SPINACH, *with Egg* 45

FRESH LAKE TROUT, Broiled, Parsley Butter, Potatoes Sauté, String Beans Fleurette.....95   LETTUCE AND CUCUMBER SALAD, Russian Dressing.....45

DELAWARE SHAD ROE, Country Bacon, Potato Chips.....95   HOT TEA BISCUITS, *with Honey*.....35

GRILLED COUNTRY HAM, Creamed New Spinach, New Potatoes.....95   FRENCH PANCAKE with Marmalade.....35

LOIN OF LAMB IN CASSEROLE *with String Beans in Butter, Parisienne Potatoes.....95*   STRAWBERRY SHORT CAKE *with Cream* 45

FRIED SPRING CHICKEN IN BUTTER, Bacon and New Potatoes in Cream.....1.25   HOME MADE PIE.....25

SMALL SIRLOIN GRILLED, *with Chives, Country Bacon and French Fried Potatoes.....1.25*   GRAPE FRUIT (Iced) HALF.....35

IMPORTED ROQUEFORT CHEESE, Toasted Crackers.....40

EGGS—Scrambled Eggs with Chopped Ham.....75
Kippered Herring on Toast, Scrambled Eggs 65
Ham and Fried Eggs 80   Bacon and Fried Eggs 80   Ham 80; (Reduced Portion) 45
Bacon 80; (Reduced Portion) 45   Baked Beans, Hot or Cold 45
Home Fried Potatoes 30   French Fried Potatoes 35   Hashed Brown Potatoes 35
Hot Asparagus, Drawn Butter 50   Asparagus Vinaigrette 50
Refugee String Beans 30   Early June Peas 30

EGGS—Omelette, Plain 60;   Ham, Bacon, Jelly or Asparagus Omelette 75
Boiled (2) 35   Scrambled 40;   with Mushroom 75   Fried (2) 40

SALADS, DESSERTS, ETC.—Pineapple and Cheese Salad, French Dressing.....45
Lettuce and Tomato Salad 45
Cream Cheese with Toasted Rye Bread and Red Currant Jelly.....40   Strawberry Preserves 35
Hawaiian Pineapple 35   Preserved Figs with Cream 50   Orange Marmalade 35
French Vanilla Ice Cream 30   Assorted Cake 25   Toast 20
Rye or Graham Bread 15; Toasted 20   Bread and Butter 15   Postum (Pot for 1) 25
Tea (Pot for 1) 25   Coffee (Pot for 1) 25   Cocoa (Pot for 1) 25   Malted Milk (Pot for One) 25
Milk (Individual Bottle) 20

Above Portions Per Person Only
An extra charge of 25 cents per person will be made for meals served out of dining car

Passengers are respectfully informed that no verbal orders for meals will be accepted, and are requested to pay the punched total only on presentation of check on which the order is written.
Please see Steward in charge of car, if the service is not entirely to your satisfaction.

J. R. SMART, Manager, Dining Service, Cincinnati, Ohio

5-B-2

Santa Fe Super Chief— Train of the Stars

Los Angeles was, for many years, a sleepy, dusty little town of no real consequence, completely overshadowed by her rich, rowdy, and glamorous neighbor to the north, San Francisco. That began to change around the turn of the nineteenth century, as a result of real estate speculation and development, the rise of the citrus industry, and the arrival of railroad "reefers"— the refrigerated cars that transported oranges, lemons, and other fresh fruit across the continent to the population centers of New York and Chicago. It was about this time, too, that California began to aggressively promote tourism, one of the state's leading industries for the past hundred years. Very early in the twentieth century, large volumes of people and cargo began to shuttle back and forth across the Southwest, and they did it by rail.

The whole Southwest was, and still is, the playpen of the Atcheson, Topeka & Sante Fe Railroad (recently merged with Burlington Northern, but that's a different book). Passengers headed from Chicago to southern California boarded one of the Santa Fe's passenger trains at Dearborn Station and rattled across the prairie and desert for three days or so. Along the way, the train made regular stops for meals at the celebrated and extremely popular Harvey House restaurants, where passengers ate themselves silly, flirted with the equally celebrated Harvey girls who served the diners, then staggered back aboard the train for a nap until it was time for the next meal. With the train averaging 40 miles per hour (64.36kph) or so—stops included—it was a leisurely way to see the country. Of course, the cars weren't air-conditioned, and the seats were fairly rigid, but it was better than riding a horse or walking, the primary alternatives back then. But they got a chance to visit with the locals and most people were not in much of a hurry at the time. All except for an odd character named Walter Scott—known for eternity as "Death Valley Scotty."

Scott was one of those people who, through no fault of his own, acquired vast riches. Scott's came from mineral deposits in California's forbidding Death Valley. He spent his money on a castle for himself out there, and on other occasional whims. And in early July, 1905, Scott wanted to go to Chicago—fast!

He commissioned the Santa Fe to take him in a special express, and paid fifty-five hundred dollars for the ride, on the condition that the trip take just forty-six hours from start to stop. Engine 442 pulled out of Santa Fe's La Grande station on Sunday, July 9, 1905, at one in the afternoon, with one passenger, Walter Scott.

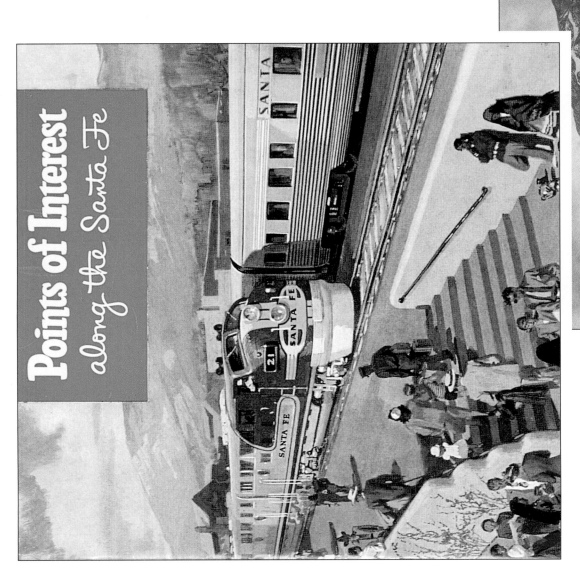

Points of Interest
along the Santa Fe

ABOVE: A vintage ad points to the Santa Fe's scenic route, drawing early-twentieth-century travelers to explore the wild, wild West.

RIGHT: A big Mountain-class locomotive with a short string of old-style passenger coaches works its way up the Cajon Pass on a steamy August morning in 1939. SF No. 3741 is one of thirty-five similar locomotives built by Baldwin between 1918 and 1924, some of which lasted a quarter century in service.

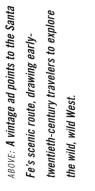

OPPOSITE: *Santa Fe No. 2903 is a World War II baby, one of thirty, now rusting in peace, if not in pieces.*

ABOVE: *Making the difficult climb up a mountain grade at the head of a long AT&SF passenger consist is a partially shrouded 4-8-4 Northern with tender, assisted by one of the most famous diesel locomotives ever built, the Super Chief.*

His consist included a baggage car, diner, and a Pullman sleeper—a light load of just 170 tons. Less than two days later, on Tuesday morning at 11:54, Scott's special glided to a halt at Chicago's Dearborn Street Station, having covered the 2,228 miles (3,584.85km) in just under forty-five hours. During the run speeds sometimes reached 100 miles per hour (160.9kph) and Scott himself sometimes assisted firing the engine.

The run got a lot of publicity, not all of it favorable, but it was a learning experience for Santa Fe. They learned that it was possible to change locomotives very quickly, for one thing, and that speed sells, for another.

Santa Fe introduced a very expensive, very exclusive passenger run in 1911, the DeLuxe. Limited to just sixty passengers, each of whom paid an extra twenty-five dollars surcharge to ride the train, the DeLuxe lived up to its name.

The first Chief entered service on November 14, 1926, as an extra-fare premier train running between Chicago and Los Angeles. By 1935, Santa Fe was running five trains a day between Chicago and the West Coast, but the Chief was the fastest and most celebrated. Movie stars often preferred it, and that glamour resulted in publicity that in turn generated ticket sales. Reservations on the Chief required a premium (twenty-five dollars during the 1950s), and the trains were generally booked solid.

The Chief glided out of Dearborn Station at eleven sharp every morning, and two days later slithered to a stop in southern California—Los Angeles at 5 PM and the end of the line, San Diego, at 9:30 PM. In between, passengers enjoyed all the amenities of a rolling hotel, with the possible exception of a swimming pool. The 1935 variant of the Chief included a club car, a barbershop, and showers for both men and women.

Like other premium passenger trains of the day, the Chief had its own dining car and kitchen, and the food was spectacular. The dining car, along with the whole train, was air-conditioned and quite elegant, but of a more traditional style than the more modern treatments found on some of the other premium passenger trains of 1935. All food preparation was under the supervision of the Fred Harvey organization and was prepared to the highest standards.

Sleeping cars were set up so that adjoining drawing rooms and compartments could be turned into suites for families or for wealthy people traveling with butlers and maids. One Pullman on the Chief of 1935 offered six compartments and three drawing rooms, while others offered variations on the same configuration.

For those women travelers who didn't have a maid of their own, Santa Fe provided one. A company brochure of the time said, "A maid travels with the train to attend to the needs of the feminine travelers." Indeed, the "Train of the Stars" provided the real star treatment.

The Chief's route was as spectacular as the food—up and over Raton Pass through Santa Fe's mile-long tunnel, down into Albuquerque and into Indian country. After World War II, Santa Fe made much of its connection with the Indians of the Southwest, particularly the Navajos, and adopted as a mascot and advertising icon a small fictitious Navajo boy named "Chico." This little boy and other Pueblo Indians frequently appeared in Santa Fe's ads during the postwar years.

Bringing up the rear of the train was an elegant parlor car, complete with a lounge just for women and children, with its own shower. The men could sit in the deeply upholstered chairs, smoke, and read the papers.

The final day of the trip found the Chief racing across the Mojave Desert, through Barstow, then through the Cajon Pass and down the steep grade into the Los Angeles basin.

Until 1936, the Chief was powered by steam. Then Santa Fe got the first of its road diesels, "boxcabs" from General Motors' Electro-Motive Corporation (EMC), and in 1937, the Chief became the Super Chief. The boxcab design looks a lot like a shoebox on wheels, and didn't last long. By 1938, Santa Fe was pulling the Super Chief with streamlined power and the wonderful "warbonnet" paint scheme applied to the new EMC E1A and E1B locomotives.

More than a locomotive, more than a railroad, the Santa Fe provided an all-encompassing travel experience for tourists at the turn of the nineteenth century. Stepping into your car on the Santa Fe meant you were "Going West" and every aspect of your travel experience—the trains, the depots, the souvenirs and even the coffee cups—were designed to enhance the sense of adventure.

This close identification of the Santa Fe with the American West did not happen all at once, but it was the conscious effort of a brilliant Santa Fe executive to create a unique travel experience. His name was Edward P. Ripley, and he was a born promoter. He took over as president of a floundering Santa Fe in

1896, and by the time he retired, twenty-five years later, he had created a legend.

Other American railroads had advertising programs complete with slogans, songs, giveaways, and gimmicks. There was Phoebe Snow, riding on the Road of Anthracite. The Rock Island Railroad had little statuettes of a traveler looking at a map designed by Rogers, a sculptor of popular, sentimental parlor pieces. Ripley went looking for a similar memorable icon.

The Santa Fe traffic manager, W. F. White, had been exploring some advertising possibilities and Ripley encouraged White to come up with a memorable promotion idea. The other key figure in marketing the Santa Fe would be William Haskell Simpson, promoted to advertising manager in 1900. Together, they would create and mold the distinctive Santa Fe identity that is now such a great part of the American West.

In the 1890s, it was decided to feature the great painting of the Grand Canyon by Sir Thomas Moran. The Santa Fe bought the rights to the Moran piece, had beautiful lithographs made, framed them in gilt

frames, and hung them by the hundreds in banks, offices, schools, hotels, and other public buildings.

Moran had first sketched the Grand Canyon twenty years earlier on a pioneering expedition with the U.S. Geodetic Survey explorer, Major John Wesley Powell. Now Moran was invited to travel once again to the rim of the canyon, this time at the expense of the Santa Fe. His painting of the Grand Canyon remains one of the most inspired paintings ever made of this glorious American vista.

By the end of the decade, the advertising department of the Santa Fe was continuing to build its art collection. Simpson continued to invite and subsidize artists who were interested in painting the West by sending them on three to four week excursions on the Santa Fe. These trips produced hundreds of paintings, drawings, and other art used by the railroad in its advertising and displayed in its depots. The Santa Fe collection of paintings would eventually grow to include over six hundred pieces.

In addition to paintings and graphic arts, the Santa Fe company was also an early and avid supporter of the manufacture of pottery, rugs, jewelry, and other work of the Native Americans of the Southwest. The railroad acquired many pieces for their collection, and Indian art was featured in the Santa Fe exhibit at the St. Louis World's Fair, held in 1904.

Although the Santa Fe encouraged artists to travel to the West, it also supported the efforts of American painters who were already working in the area. Art colonies in Santa Fe and Taos began forming in the 1890s, and after the turn of the century, the railroad regularly bought paintings from local artists. The railroad featured their works in their famous calendar, a promotional project that was initiated in 1907.

Calendars were printed and distributed by the hundreds of thousands, so selection as a Santa Fe calendar artist was an incredible accolade.

In addition to the Santa Fe advertising and print campaigns featuring the art of the American West, the famous Harvey House restaurant chain also used Western and Native American motifs in their establishments. Harvey House restaurants became synonymous with the Santa Fe railroad during its early days. The high quality of the food and the pleasant waitresses, as well as the prompt and efficient service, made the Harvey Houses famous around the world.

There was such a close relationship between Santa Fe and the Harvey House chain that the experience became a unified one for the traveler. Many of the Santa Fe depots along the line were designed by architect Charles F. Whittlesey, a designer who is now credited with rekindling interest in the pueblo style. Interested in local architecture, Whittlesey designed railroad depots that recalled the buildings of the early Spanish explorers.

Whittlesey was a native of Alton, Illinois, and was trained in architecture in the Chicago office of Louis Sullivan. Sullivan was the mentor of another extremely original American architect, Frank Lloyd Wright. In 1900, Mr. Whittlesey was appointed Chief Architect of the Santa Fe Railroad, and was in charge of building the hotels and depots along the line. His notable designs would include the Alvarado Hotel, the Station in Albuquerque, and the magnificent El Tovar Hotel at the Grand Canyon, built to resemble a pueblo village.

Another key designer who shaped the Santa Fe experience was designer and architect Mary E.J. Colter. She was also a Midwesterner, a native of Kansas City, Missouri. Perhaps more than any other designer, Colter was responsible for implementing the design details that made the Santa Fe experience so memorable. She chose or designed the unique Southwestern style furniture, light fixtures, and textiles used in the hotels and shops to implement a particular design theme.

The motifs on the china used in the Santa Fe dining cars, now highly sought after by collectors, were her choices. She was also a great enthusiast of Native American art and helped promote the sales of rugs, pottery, and other crafts. The Santa Fe railroad and Fred Harvey alliance was unique among American railroads because many of its stations included a gift shop and studio adjacent to the depot, where Native American work was sold. The gift shops were designed as part of the station complex.

It has been said that Fred Harvey and the Santa Fe can be credited with introducing America to Americans. Carrying the support for local artists one step further, space for artists' studios was incorporated into the gift shops and larger hotels. To ensure a continued support for genuine Navajo rugs and other artifacts, the Harvey chain purchased thousands of machine-made textiles and labeled them as imitations.

OPPOSITE LEFT: Pullman-Standard's dome car featured tremendous visibility thanks to the many windows, and plenty of comfort thanks to the swiveling armchairs.

OPPOSITE RIGHT: Here, the 2-8-8-2 No. 1792 of the Norfolk & Western assists the westbound Chief up Raton Pass near Trinidad, Colorado.

ABOVE: Not long before steam evaporated from the Santa Fe, this passenger train is propelled by a big Northern steamer with its whistle blasting, coming around a curve near Summit, California.

RIGHT: Santa Fe tried all sorts of diesel designs on its premium passenger runs, including these ALCO PA-1 locomotives, the first of the breed for that railroad. PA-1s would haul the Super Chief and El Capitans over the years but would never come close to the popularity of EMD's E model.

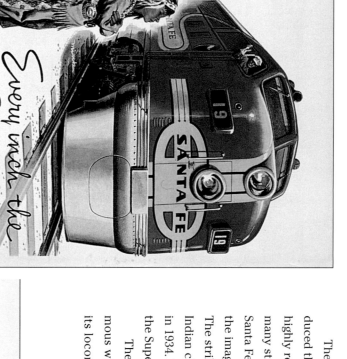

The Santa Fe Railway art program eventually produced the portrait of an Indian chief that became such a highly recognized symbol. Artist E. Irving Couse painted many strong images of Native Americans for the annual Santa Fe calendar. But it took until the mid-1930s before the image known as The Santa Fe Indian came into being.

The striking portrait by Couse, featuring the profile of an Indian chief wearing a feathered warbonnet, was produced in 1934. It would give an immortal name to a classic train, the Super Chief.

The warbonnet paint scheme would become synonymous with Santa Fe, and variations have been applied to its locomotives until quite recently, a very handsome and dramatic graphic treatment for the hood of a locomotive. Along with the young Navajo boy, the warbonnet paint scheme helped identify Santa Fe in the public's mind, giving the railway a unique and decidedly Southwestern personality that set it apart from the more cosmopolitan lines of the East.

This graphic treatment was the product of two extremely talented men, Electro-Motive Corporation's (EMC) Leland Knickerbocker and industrial designer Sterling McDonald. McDonald came up with the Southwestern theme, and Knickerbocker, EMC's color specialist, put the theme into bright red and yellow forms suggestive of a Plains Indian's warbonnet.

ABOVE: Advertisements for the Sante Fe line emphasized the Native-American heritage of the American Southwest.

RIGHT: By 1938, big, gaudy diesels like this E2A from Electro-Motive Corporation were the hottest things on the rails. Diesels proved their superiority on the vast desert territory of the Santa Fe, and it wasn't long before flashy locomotives like No. 9 were attracting a lot of attention with their handsome red and yellow "warbonnet" paint scheme.

OPPOSITE: The Super Chief with a handsome EMD locomotive on the point.

Southern Pacific

The Beautiful Daylights

One of the most beautiful and memorable of all the classic passenger train runs has to be Southern Pacific's several Daylights. There were several of these, all West Coast trains catering to a tourist market.

The first and foremost was the Coast Daylight, inaugurated on March 21, 1937, to run between Los Angeles and San Francisco along a 471-mile (757.84km) route. The route, which closely paralleled the Pacific Coast for 115 miles (185.04km) of spectacular scenery was one part of the draw, but the other draw was the train itself, a fast, elegant, comfortable operation designed to draw tourists and natives alike.

Train service along the coast was old news by 1937. Southern Pacific (SP) had offered a slow, Spartan train called the Coastline Limited beginning in 1901. That trip took almost fifteen hours—if and when the train was on time—and offered just chair cars. More comfortable parlor cars were added five years later.

Then came the Daylight Limited in 1922 with a special schedule—only in the summer and only on Friday and Saturday, but now with a diner car. This crack express covered the route in thirteen hours flat, but at the expense of not a single station stop to pick up or drop off passengers. There was a howl of protest from places like Santa Barbara and San Luis Obispo, both catering to a tourist crowd themselves, and SP relented. Even so, the Daylight Limited was Southern Pacific's fastest train.

The Daylight was quite successful that first year, so much so that another train was added on Sundays. But three days a week wasn't enough for the marketplace, and demand for the service was so great that Southern Pacific made the train a daily on a year-round schedule in July. Soon it had a dining car and an observation car with a huge platform for all the people intent on enjoying the scenery—as many as thirty-two, far more than conventional observation platforms.

Southern Pacific was notoriously conservative about all aspects of its operation, but the Daylight gradually became the railroad's flagship train. Lord & Thomas, the SP's advertising agency, encouraged the adoption of the Budd Company's lightweight, streamlined, stainless steel equipment on the run, just as so many other companies were doing with their own premier passenger trains. The idea was rejected in favor of conventional heavy Pullman-built cars of the best style and substance, and the order was placed in March 1936.

The newly transformed Daylight was promoted and publicized with all the intensity and excess for which the 1930s were famous. A color scheme of black, silver, red, and orange was selected, tested, and approved. Two full sets of cars were ordered at a cost of a million dollars each, along with orders to Lima for six new 4-6-4 Northern-class locomotives at a cost of more than a million.

In March 1937, Southern Pacific began checking out the new equipment with trial runs along the route, just to make sure the new Lima GS-2 power was up to

*OPPOSITE: **Southern Pacific's No. 4449 appears out of the mist, producing some mist of its own. A flagship locomotive of the Northern type, 4449 and its sisters powered SP's premier trains during the 1940s and '50s, including the Daylights, up and down the California coast, and all the way up into Oregon and Washington.***

*LEFT: **The "Last Daylight," Southern Pacific No. 4449, halts at one of the old "Coast Daylight's" regular stops, Paso Robles, California, with a railfan excursion train in tow.***

*ABOVE: **A vintage ad for SP's Daylights boasts, "The World's Most Beautiful Trains—The World's Most Beautiful Trip."***

ABOVE: *Southern Pacific's* West *magazine investigated all the scenic destinations along its signature line.*

RIGHT: *SP No. 4449 returns to the same tracks out in the California central valley where she and her sisters used to run back in the 1950s with the Shasta Daylight.*

LEFT: Two grand old ladies of an earlier era ready for a night of adventure: SP No. 4449, a beautifully restored Northern type, and SP No. 2472, a Pacific, await their orders. Both these locomotives represent the best of the modern locomotive preservation movement and the many thousands of hours of free labor by volunteers.

BELOW: A vintage advertisement sings the praises of Pullman's cars for SP's Daylights.

getting the heavy train over the steep Cuesta Grade north of San Luis Obispo. The GS was an abbreviation for "Golden State," and these were supposed to be the most muscular and agile streamlined steam locomotives ever manufactured.

SP claimed that the new train, each consist of which represented a million dollars of outlay, was "the most beautiful train in the West." Then they changed that claim to "the most beautiful train in the world." Finally, after many press releases and much hot air, SP train No. 99, the Coast Daylight, was ready for its first revenue run from Los Angeles. NBC carried the festivities live beginning at seven in the morning, and at eight fifteen, Olivia de Havilland did the christening honors with a bottle of champagne and the northbound Daylight was off.

Up in San Francisco, the southbound train was also preparing to leave, but without as much fanfare.

That southbound run made headlines, too—the most passengers carried on a single train, the most food and drink served, and, best of all, the most profit-per-mile of any train on record.

A typical Daylight could hold about 465 passengers, and the typical Daylight was stuffed to the gills with them. Ridership on the Daylight was amazing—eighteen thousand the first month of operation, twenty-four thousand the next, a million and a half in the first year. People loved the scenery; they loved the fully reclining seats; and they loved the food and service. Other railroads might feature massive steaks on their menu, but the classic dish on the Daylight and every other SP train with a diner was the legendary SP Salad. Forty-five people worked each train, a staff to passenger ratio of about one to ten, much lower than on other trains. During the first months of operation, the consist included the normal combination baggage and chair car at the head end, then three chair cars, a tavern and coffee shop car, a diner, and a parlor car, all followed up by an elegant observation car on the end of the train.

SP added two tavern cars and two coffee shop cars to the rolling stock, but that wasn't enough. Second sections were common to accommodate the overflow demand for travel on the train, but only the first section got the deluxe treatment.

Now the Daylight was up to fourteen cars, and ridership of almost four hundred passengers on average. SP bought more locomotives, more cars, and more advertising. Cars and locomotives were pilfered from less popular runs and dragooned for service on the Daylight.

During World War II, the Daylight equipment got a workout—about a million passengers a year, and around thirty-five hundred per day toward the end. After the war, things got slowly back to normal. SP capitalized on the success of the Coast Daylight and developed several other versions of the popular concept, including the Shasta Daylight (running through the Cascades up to Portland, Oregon) introduced in 1947.

Diesels replaced the grand Lima GS steamers in 1955, but ridership was off and so was the quality of what had been SP's premier train. The consist dropped to eleven cars on many days, and even those were seldom full. Two more cars were removed in 1959. SP kept the Coast Daylight in operation all through the 1960s, but in a deteriorating, pathetic way, with ancient rolling stock and a mixed bag of whatever locomotives might be available. The lights went out for the Daylight when Amtrak took over mainline passenger operations in the United States in 1971.

RIGHT: 4449 is one of a hundred or so steam locomotives still in irregular passenger service around the United States and Canada. Operating such a locomotive on mainlines that have long since abandoned coaling towers and water tanks is quite a challenge.

SOUTHERN PACIFIC'S SIMPLE SIGNATURE SALAD

While other railroads might boast of their elaborate dollar dinners, their specialty prime rib ends, their fresh dinner rolls, and other culinary delights, Southern Pacific's patrons were always careful to order the SP Salad Bowl, no matter what else they might select from the menu. Southern Pacific's freight business serviced California and Arizona's extensive agriculture industry, so it is no surprise that SP's produce was fresh. Still, fresh lettuce wasn't as common in the 1920s, '30s, and '40s as it is today, and the Salad Bowl was extremely popular. The basic components are simple enough, although the special SP Dressing was a little quirky and passengers demanded to know how to make it at home. Southern Pacific wasn't shy about the recipe and included it in brochures promoting the line's deluxe passenger runs. Here it is:

Take two heads of extremely fresh iceberg lettuce and tear into small bite-sized pieces. Immerse four large, firm, fresh tomatoes in boiling water for sixty seconds, then place them in cold water momentarily and peel the skins off. Quarter the tomatoes and add to the lettuce. Add half a bunch of radishes, thinly sliced, and a cucumber, peeled, scored, and thinly sliced. Sprinkle one teaspoon of sugar over it all, and finally, add one green bell pepper that has been cored, seeded, sliced in strips, and shredded.

The salad is dressed with Southern Pacific Dressing—a cup of mayonnaise, a cup of ketchup, half a cup of currant jelly, a heaping teaspoon of dry mustard, and a level teaspoon of salt. Dissolve the mustard and salt in a bit of vinegar—just enough to do the job—then add the other ingredients and mix till blended. This is enough for several salads.

The Southern Pacific Salad Bowl was presented in a Prairie Mountain Wildflower Syracuse salad bowl, and was one of the most popular items in the diner of the Sunset Limited, the Overland, and all of the Daylights.

SUNSET LIMITED *to* **California**

ABOVE AND RIGHT: **Dining service on board Southern Pacific's passenger lines boasted the bounty of fresh produce coming out of California and Arizona, and no item was as popular as SP's signature salad.**

LOUNGE and BUFFET SERVICE

Chicago, Burlington & Quincy's (CB&Q) Pioneer Zephyr

Early on a crisp May morning in 1934, standing amid a crowd on the platform of Denver's cavernous Union Station, Mr. C. J. Ince, the general manager for Western Union's Western Division, looked up into the cab of a very new and unusual locomotive, caught the eye of its engineer, and ceremoniously dropped a flag, signaling the start of a race against the clock.

The train was the Chicago, Burlington & Quincy's (CB&Q) new Zephyr, a short little consist made up of just three cars and one engine, and it was about to prove a point and transform an industry. The engineer advanced his throttle and instead of the deep, rhythmic heartbeat of a steam engine, the crowd listened to the song of a new kind of power, the steady, rising whine of a diesel engine and the hum of a generator. As the locomotive began to move, it broke a tape attached to a special clock installed to set the start time for the run—05:04:40. The engineer eased his train slowly out of Denver, Colorado's Union Station, past the excited crowds, then through the yards, and accelerated out onto the mainline, eastbound on a run that everybody present knew would make the headlines and history books.

The Zephyr was revolutionary, from the wheels up. The entire train was designed and built as a set, using gleaming lightweight stainless steel, and streamlined in a sleek, aerodynamic way, based on wind tunnel testing and careful calculations. But the real revolution was out of sight, under the long hood of the engine. Inside, providing motive power, was a 660hp diesel engine driving a generator wired to massive electrical motors that were geared to the driving wheels. Diesel power had been used in locomotives for fifteen years at that point, but for slow-speed switching operations, not for high-speed passenger runs. That was about to change.

Burlington, the train's owner, developed the Zephyr for the relatively short but potentially profitable run from Kansas City up to Omaha and Lincoln, Nebraska, and commissioned the Budd Car Company to build the train as an efficient, economical alternative to the two locomotives and six-car consists then in use. But before placing it in revenue service, Burlington decided that the new train deserved some special publicity, and somebody came up with the idea of a fast run across the prairie—and a lot farther than from Kansas City to Lincoln.

Instead, the Zephyr was going to make a try for a new speed and endurance record. Burlington's normal high-speed train for the Denver-Chicago route was the Aristocrat, and its scheduled run for the 1,015 miles (1,633.14km) was a respectably brief twenty-five hours and forty-five minutes, stops included. The Zephyr had been getting attention even before this attempt by racing airplanes and beating them, but this race was even more important.

Publicity for the run had been intense, and so had the preparation. For months, the papers had

OPPOSITE: The Silver King and Silver Queen locomotives were used to power the ten-car Pioneer Zephyr on its rapid runs between Chicago and Denver during the mid 1930s.

ABOVE: Sixty years after its triumphal run from Denver to Chicago, the Pioneer Zephyr is well preserved and undergoing restoration.

RIGHT: One of the signal pleasures of traveling by train is watching the scenery flash by. For this father and daughter on the California Zephyr, the views are truly breathtaking.

included stories about the race between UP and CB&Q's new concept trains. For weeks, the papers had been running glowing accounts of UP's futuristic, teardrop-shaped M10000. For days, the newspapers had been full of articles about the run, and about the Burlington's preparation for the record-setting attempt. Track crews had been busy for days repairing defects in ballast, rail, and switches. Difficult sections of track were patrolled by the Burlington's crews, watching for any possible sabotage by competing railroads or anybody else. The public was fascinated.

As the Zephyr glided out of Denver, down the long, gradual slope of the western great plains, every other train on the line was ordered out of the way, onto sidings, to let this glittering, polished steel creature breeze past.

Crowds lined the platform of every station, and lined the whole right of way. Everybody who could dropped what they were doing and went down to the track to see the new train make its run at the history books. Farmers in their fields stopped their plowing to gawk along with everybody else.

Aboard the Zephyr was a small horde of newspaper reporters and Burlington executives, along with three engineers. Ralph Budd, president of the CB&Q, was aboard, along with most of the senior officers of the line, H. L. Hamilton (president of the company that built the diesel engine), and a small platoon of technicians ready to repair any problem with the train—plus a burro named Zeph, brought along as a mascot at the suggestion of President Budd.

It isn't very often that an engineer gets the mainline to himself, every signal green, every signal a high-ball, every signal reporting "clear block," but that's what the Zephyr's pilots saw on that momentous day. Opening the throttle, the train accelerated . . . 60, 70, 80 miles per hour (95.54, 112.63, and 128.72kph, respectively), and stayed there. Capable of 120 miles per hour (193.08kph), the Zephyr was limited by speed restrictions of the roadbed rather than the machine.

Until that day, the record run for a locomotive over a four hundred mile (643.6km) course had been achieved by the powerful steam engine Royal Scotsman running between London and Glasgow six years earlier, in 1928. It took six hours and fifty-seven minutes, an average speed of 56 miles per hour (91.1kph) The Zephyr whacked almost two full hours off that record, making the run from Denver to Harvard, Nebraska, in just over four hours and at an average speed of almost 80 miles per hour (128.72kph). The train maintained a speed of nearly 100 miles per hour (106.9kph) for an hour and a half, and at one point, accelerated to over 112 miles per hour (119.73kph) on a three-mile section of smooth, straight track.

Until that day, locomotives had to stop every 100 miles (106.9km) or so for water and coal, but not the Zephyr—it roared past every water tank and coal tower without slowing down, its 600 gallons (2,280L) of fuel more than enough to make it to Chicago.

The engineer for the last leg of the trip was J. S. Ford, who took over for the final 165 miles (265.49km), and at nine minutes past eight, he eased the Zephyr to a halt before another crowd, this time in Chicago's Halsted Street Station. The run had lasted thirteen hours and five minutes for the 1,015 miles (1,633.12km)—almost two hours faster than expected, almost twice as fast as the competition. A crowd of about 100,000 people cheered the train a few hours later when it was carefully moved to be put on display at the Century of Progress Exposition.

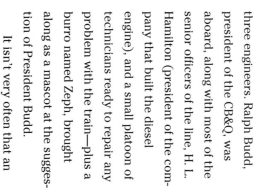

LEFT: *The Zephyr's pioneering diesel-electric power train and unique stainless steel construction were played up in ads for the Chicago, Burlington, & Quincy lines.*

ABOVE: *The head end of the Pioneer Zephyr during restoration. The restoration was completed in 1997; the train is now part of the Museum of Science and Industry in Chicago, Illinois.*

OPPOSITE: *The shiny steel exterior that defined the Pioneer Zephyr inspired more than just oohs and ahhs. Its mirror-like finish was perfect for last minute primping.*

As intended, the run got the attention of both the public and the railroad industry. People flocked to see the Zephyr as it toured the country after the exposition, visiting thirty-one states and more than two hundred cities. But the real excitement was within the industry: the run from Denver to Chicago was made for a fuel cost of just over seventeen dollars, and the train's operating expenses worked out to only thirty-four cents per mile, about half the cost of operation for a steam-powered train on the same run. The diesel proved to be economical and reliable, which, combined with the high speeds and great popularity of the new technology, helped create tremendous interest in diesel power throughout the industry.

The Zephyr finally went into revenue service between Kansas City and Lincoln, Nebraska, on November 11, 1934 and continued to be efficient, economical, popular . . . and then profitable. On the first day of service, returning to Kansas City, several auto drivers tried to race the train on roads parallel to the tracks, but the Zephyr just left them flapping in its wake, accelerating easily to 80 miles per hour (128.72kph) and breezing back to Union Station.

Demand for the seventy-two seats on the train was so great that many people were turned away. A fourth coach with a buffet and forty more seats was added, and at the same time the smoking section of one of the original cars was converted to store baggage. Now the Zephyr carried ninety-two passengers, pulling 50 percent more passengers than the previous train, Pride of the Prairie, at half the cost per mile.

Burlington added several other Zephyrs, among the most famous of which was the California Zephyr, but the original soldiered on for another twenty-six years. Re-christened the Pioneer Zephyr, it made its last run from Lincoln, Nebraska, to Galesburg, Illinois, on March 20, 1960. A few days later, exactly twenty-six years to the day it rewrote railroad history and after 3.25 million miles (5,229,250km) of service, the Zephyr glided back into downtown Chicago to be presented to the Museum of Science and Industry.

California Zephyr (CZ)

Nobody really knew for sure what would happen to the passenger rail business after World War II. The railroads were hoping they could pick up where they left off in 1942, and had promoted rail all during the war, even when they could do little about their quality of service. Even so, they made big plans for new equipment and services to replace the packed, dirty, worn-out equipment that served during the war. *Life* and all the other magazines were loaded with full-page ads describing the passenger trains of the postwar era, and those advertisements showed an exciting future.

One of the trains that fulfilled that promise was the California Zephyr, among the premiere operations of the late '40s and '50s. There were many Zephyrs after 1934, and all of them were great trains, but the one that ran between San Francisco and Chicago was famous in its day and is revered today by those that rode it and by those who wish they had.

Part of its vast appeal was the route. You could have put people in folding chairs on a flatcar and hauled them across the country behind the Toonerville Trolley, and they would have been thrilled if it went along the route of the CZ. That route was refreshingly different for anybody who'd been across on the Chief, through the Southwest, or on the City of San Francisco, up and over Donner Pass. The CZ departed Oakland, California, paused briefly at Sacramento, then turned left up the eastern side of California's fertile valley, and began to climb upward into the tall ponderosa pines along the spectacular Feather River. Then it was over the Sierras and into Nevada's

great desert for the race toward Salt Lake City, Utah, during the night where Western Pacific's locomotive was exchanged for one owned by the Denver & Rio Grand Western (DRG&W).

Passengers spent the second day out with their noses pressed against the Vista Dome glass, marveling at the sweep and majesty of the Rocky Mountains. The tracks turned south, through Provo, Utah, then to Helper (a town named for the "helper" locomotives that gave trains a boost over the steep grades), on to Grand Junction, Glenwood Springs, Colorado and then through the Moffat Tunnel at the top of the railroading world, and then down the steep eastern slope of the Rockies into Denver. Here, CB&Q took over for the final dash across the plains with momentary pauses at McCook, Hastings, and Omaha, Nebraska, before crossing Iowa and Illinois. About two and a half days out of Oakland, the CZ glided to its moorings in Chicago.

The CZ was the joint product of several railroads—the Western Pacific, Denver & Rio Grande Western, and the dear old Chicago, Denver & Quincy—with a big helping of genius from C.R. Osborn. Osborn was the general manager for General Motors' (GM) Electro-Motive Division, the old EMC that was now a subsidiary of the giant automobile builder.

Osborn got a "cab ride" in one of his new diesel locomotives up Glenwood Canyon on July 4, 1944, just to check out his company's product, but he was tremendously impressed with the view. He noticed that he could enjoy the scenery and the ride much better from his perch up in the cab than in even the most luxurious seat back in the cars. He, better than almost anyone, was aware of the pressures on the industry and the demand for innovative ways to attract passengers back to trains after the war, and he had an idea that would soon become the Vista Dome.

LEFT: During the later years of its existence, the California Zephyr got conventional lightweight equipment, including the Silver Lariat dome car, currently on display at the California State Railroad Museum at Sacramento.

ABOVE: A timetable for the Denver & Rio Grand Western Railroad lured passengers West with promises of five views of the majestic Rocky Mountains.

OPPOSITE: The 1936 Denver Zephyr was modern in every way, the complete antithesis of the heavy, stodgy cars of an earlier era. Lost was the platform on the back of the observation car, but it was replaced with a wonderful panoramic view.

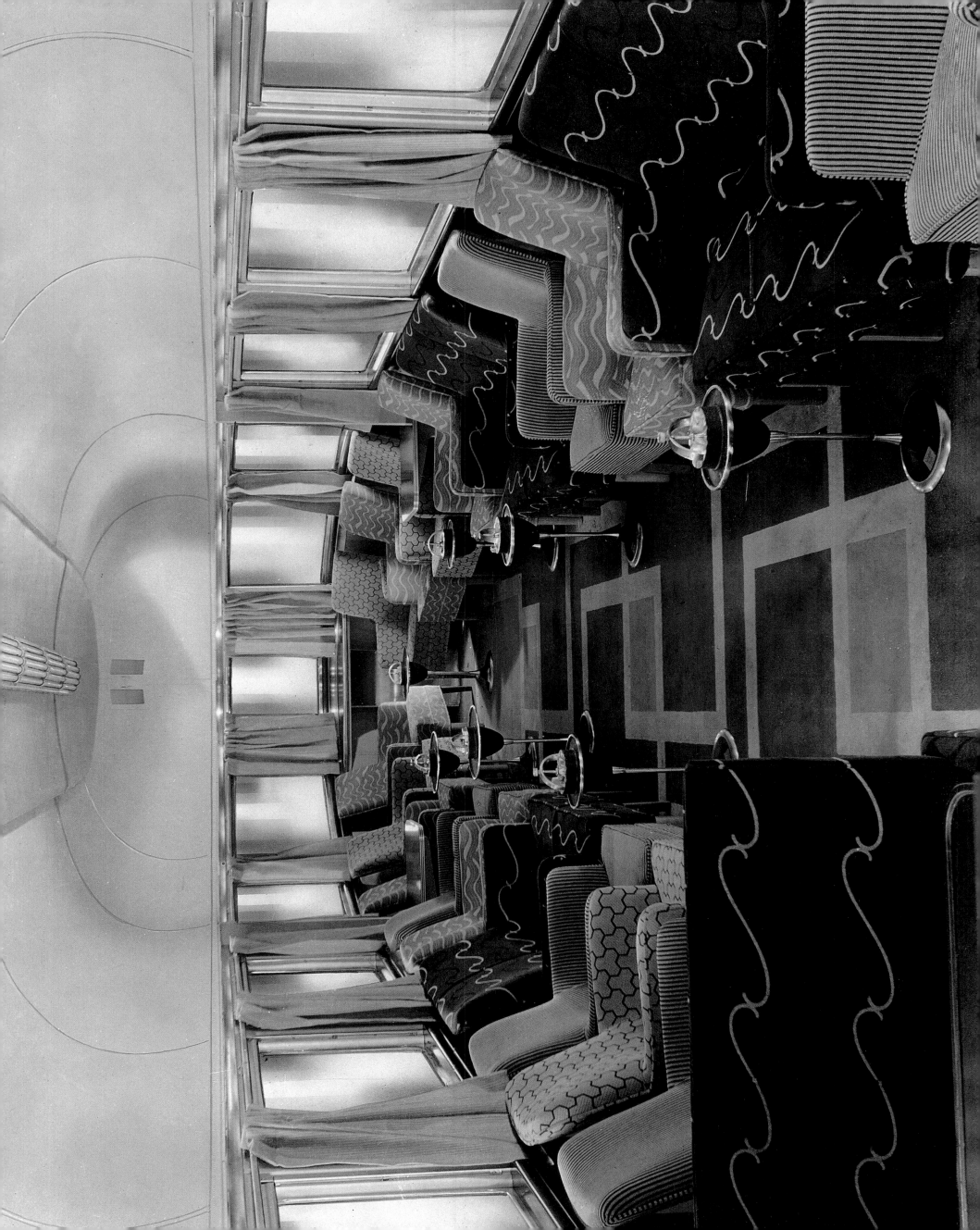

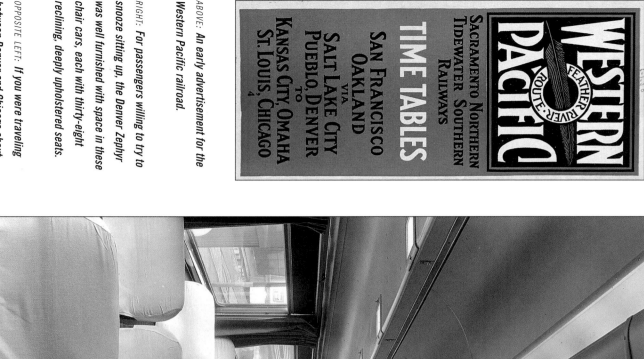

ABOVE: An early advertisement for the Western Pacific railroad.

RIGHT: For passengers willing to try to snooze sitting up, the Denver Zephyr was well furnished with space in these chair cars, each with thirty-eight reclining, deeply upholstered seats.

OPPOSITE LEFT: If you were traveling between Denver and Chicago about 1936, you'd be assigned to a section like this—comfortable seats during the day, slightly lumpy bunks at night.

OPPOSITE RIGHT: The Zephyr's diner was as clean, simple, and elegant as the rest of the train but still managed to turn out excellent food for its patrons.

Osborn turned EMD's engineers loose on his idea for a special observation car. They took an old, conventional Budd chair car, gutted it, and added something that looked like a green house or perhaps a very big canopy from a very large airplane. Under this canopy, they installed seats that put passengers up about 10 feet (3.05m) higher than normal with an almost unobstructed 360-degree view. It was the ultimate sightseeing device, and it turned out to be an immediate hit.

GM had a big stake in the postwar rail industry and promoted their role with the Train of Tomorrow, a collection of innovations on wheels, right after the war. The Train of Tomorrow toured the country and looked just like all the gee-whiz, Buck Rogers concoctions that everybody had seen in the ads. They flocked to see it, and they loved the observation dome cars perhaps more than anything.

Western Pacific had been planning a premier Zephyr train even before the war; now they could put it in service. After negotiating a deal with the CB&Q and DRG&W, each of whom would be partly responsible for the train, new Vista Dome cars were ordered from Budd in 1945. Other trains were ordering Osborn's dome cars, but the CZ would have the most—five in each consist, all stainless steel and as shiny and brilliant as a B-29. Each of the new Zephyrs would have ten new cars, including the Vista Domes, but then the order was bumped up to eleven, then thirteen cars in each train, all based on the expectation of high demand for the service.

The first complete California Zephyr was christened on Saturday, the nineteenth of March, 1949. The president of Western Pacific made a speech, the governor of the state made a speech, and then Miss Eleanor Parker, a beautiful and dewy-eyed starlet from Warner Brothers, busted a bottle of expensive champagne against the prow of the new locomotive (an EMD F3 No. 802), saying, "I christen thee the California Zephyr!"

The next day, Sunday, March 20, the first CZ departed from Oakland, across the bay, at precisely

9:30 AM. All the female passengers were presented with silver orchids flown in from Hawaii and the Western Pacific band played.

The Vista Dome cars were a tremendous success and perfectly suited to the route of this train. The scenic parts of the 2,525 mile (4,062.73km) run were traversed in daylight, the Nevada desert and Great Plains at night. Passengers could actually look up from their seats at the trees and mountains of the Feather River gorge and across the Rockies, all in air-conditioned comfort. It was a revelation for old-time travelers, and a great success.

Train No. 17, running the return trip, left Chicago at 3:30 PM. Passengers sat down to dinner while the rich farmland of Iowa streamed past the windows and were in Denver about breakfast time. Daylight hours were spent traversing the Rockies, and at 10:05 PM passengers working on their third or fourth

highball might or might not notice Salt Lake City's Union Station outside the windows during a twenty-minute halt. Here, the WP's power took over from D&GRW. About six in the morning, at first light, the CZ rolled across the California state line and up into the Sierras for another day of sightseeing, and at 4:15 that afternoon, the CZ eased to a halt in Oakland, the end of the line.

Accommodations were excellent during the CZ's golden years during the 1950s. A typical car included six double bedrooms and five private compartments. Each room had its own lavatory, sound system with radio and recorded music options, and chilled water. Venetian blinds covered the windows, and the seats were fully adjustable.

Although the consist varied quite a bit during the CZ's history, here is how the train was made up in the

1950s: first, a baggage car, then three Vista Dome chair coaches, a combination Dome-Lounge-Buffet, then the dining and kitchen cars, four sleeping cars, and a Vista Dome observation and lounge car bringing up the end.

By 1960, though, the culture had changed. Everybody owned cars and now the interstate highway system was being completed at a rapid rate. Before the war, driving across the country was an ordeal. After about 1955, it was a new adventure, somewhat akin to taking a plane. Both air and high-way systems sucked the air out of the passenger rail environment after 1960, and in 1965 Western Pacific applied to have the CZ service terminated. The request was denied, but in 1968, it was finally approved. One of the favorite trains of all time was retired.

LEFT: At the head end of the Zephyr would be found this charming oasis of liquid refreshment and friendly companionship in the lounge. Equipped with luxurious seating and a wide variety of wines, beers, and spirits, the lounge was a favorite place to spend an hour or two during the rapid run from one city to another.

BELOW: It was a sensational train in many ways and changed railroading in the United States forever: the Pioneer Zephyr in all its 1934 glory.

THE ZEPHYRETTES

One of the attractions of the CZ was its inclusion on the crew from the very first run of several young female attendants, the Zephyrettes. Many of the best trains included the services of female attendants, often in the form of one or more maids. The CZ, however, emulated the airlines' stewardesses in a program designed and supervised by Velma McPeak.

Burlington had a tradition of such service, first on the Chicago to Denver Zephyrs. They answered questions, took dinner reservations, helped passengers send telegrams, and made announcements over the public address system.

These young women were far more than maids. Attired in very handsome and stylish uniforms—the winter version before World War II included a cape lined in red silk—the Zephyrettes managed to look very attractive and authoritative at the same time. They paid extra attention to the needs of women traveling with children, a large part of the potential market for the CZ after the war.

An applicant was expected to be a college graduate, single, in her mid-twenties, between 5 1/3 feet (162.56cm) and 5 2/3 feet (172.72cm) tall, and with "good character and pleasing personality." She was also admonished to "...conduct herself with dignity and poise, and avoid any familiarities and acceptance of invitations from passengers or employees of the railroads. The Zephyrette is not permitted to drink or smoke while in uniform, and she must avoid spending time with passengers when they are drinking."

LEFT: The Zephyrettes were more educated and authoritative than the maids employed by other lines, and unlike the Sante Fe's Harvey Girls, they worked on the trains rather than at the stations.

Hiawatha on the Warpath

The route from Chicago up to the twin cities of Minneapolis and St. Paul is a fairly short one, only about 400 miles (643.6km), but the competition for traffic on the line was intense back in the mid-1930s. There was enough traffic, in fact, that in 1935, the Milwaukee Road introduced a radical new trainset, a sleek, extremely fast, Speedliner christened the Hiawatha.

Designed to compete head to head with the Chicago, Burlington & Quincy's new and very popular diesel Zephyr, then running between the two metropolitan areas on a six and a half hour schedule at an average speed of 66.3 miles per hour (106.68kph), the Hiawatha retained steam power, but in a new form.

The "power on the point" was a beautiful ALCO (American Locomotive Company) Type 4-4-2 A-class Atlantic, the very first "streamlined" steam locomotives and the first designed to operate at sustained speeds of over 100 miles per hour (106.9kph). Only four of these were built, the first specifically for Hiawatha service, and they were modern in every detail.

The exterior of the locomotive was carefully faired to reduce aerodynamic drag, and even the drivers were partially enclosed by the smooth superstructure. Fueled with oil instead of coal, the engine needed to stop far less often. Its Alemite lube system eliminated the requirement for the crew to walk around filling oil cups at every halt, another efficiency. Much of the locomotive's construction was of welded rather than riveted steel, making the engine both strong and light. And roller bearings, another new feature, were fitted to every wheel on the whole train, decreasing rolling resistance and improving reliability. With boiler pressures of 300 psi, huge 19-inch (48.26cm) diameter cylinders, and drivers 7 feet (2.13m) high, these locomotives were bred for speed, and they were capable of 120 miles per hour (193.08kph).

Six lightweight all-steel cars comprised the trailing load. Each was developed by the Milwaukee Road for the Hiawatha, and all included more innovative features like air-conditioning, rubber-mounted trucks, and sound-absorbing panels.

Directly behind the immense tender was the first car of the train, the restaurant and buffet car with its full kitchen. Within this car was the Tip Top Tap Room, a swank bar where passengers could get a drink or a meal anytime during the whole trip. Adjacent to the bar was a separate restaurant section where elegant full-service meals were offered.

Right behind the dining car were three luxurious passenger cars and two elegant parlor cars. Seats were deeply cushioned, with backs that reclined for a comfortable nap. Overhead were spacious luggage racks and diffused lighting that could be controlled by individual passengers. For those who didn't feel like visiting the bar for serious refreshments, a water cooler at the end of the car provided chilled, filtered water, another luxury feature of the time.

Two parlor cars brought up the rear of the train, both with reserved seating only. These parlor cars were exceptionally roomy and equipped with a smoking room for gentlemen and a lounge for the ladies. Each of these little refuges offered deeply upholstered sofas, tidy wash basins, and toilet facilities. They also offered a place where passengers could smoke and visit without bothering others. The last of these parlor cars had a distinctive "beaver-tail" shape that reduced the suction created by the passage of the train through the air at high speed.

All this elegant styling was the product of Otto Kuhler, one of the great early industrial designers, and the Hiawatha was his highest achievement. He helped transform the popular notion of what a locomotive should look like with his use of smooth, glittering stainless steel shrouding, painted with maroon, gray, and bright orange accents.

An idealized view of the Railroad Fair to be held on Chicago's lakefront, July 20-Sept.7.

New Hiawatha to star at CHICAGO RAILROAD FAIR

This summer millions will attend a brilliant exposition celebrating railroad progress. A new Twin Cities HIAWATHA will add luster to this history-making Centennial.

We invite you to inspect examples of Milwaukee Road car building. A fine specimen that will be on display is the car pictured here. Its distinctive Skytop Lounge is an observation room designed for more enjoyable sightseeing. These Skytop Lounges are on the AM and PM Twin Cities HIAWATHAS, and cars of similar type will be on the Olympian HIAWATHA.

With 153 new cars now being delivered, the Milwaukee Road will amplify its HIAWATHA services. Soon the Hiawatha fleet will be operating nine thousand miles a day. It's a Hiawatha year! H. Sengstacken, Passenger Traffic Manager, 708 Union Station, Chicago 6, Illinois.

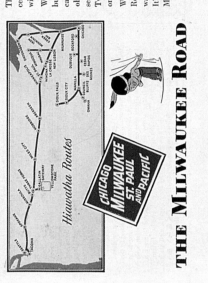

Hiawatha Routes

CHICAGO MILWAUKEE ST. PAUL and PACIFIC

THE MILWAUKEE ROAD

OPPOSITE: **One of the most handsome streamlined locomotives, the lightweight Hiawatha was also one of the few built in-house by a railroad's own car shop.**

ABOVE: **Advertisements for the Milwaukee Road's Hiawatha line made much of the trains' skytop lounge cars.**

Rails Across the
Great White North

Canadians and Americans share a lot of heritage and a lot of customs, but things are always a little different on the northern side of the border, often in special, charming ways. The Confederation of Canada was formed in 1867, unifying what had been (and still sometimes are) quite independent provinces. But it wasn't until nearly the end of the nineteenth century that rail travel between British Columbia in the west and the provinces to the east was finally possible.

Although Canada's cultural ties with Britain are strong, her trade and technology have long been enmeshed with those of the United States. As a result, Canada's railroads have what looks to be an American foundation, but with a special Canadian twist.

Baldwin sold lots of 4-4-0 "American" locomotives to Canadian railroads during the formative years of that nation and her railroads, and Pullman supplied a lot of sleeping cars, too. But Canadian factories like Montreal Locomotive Works turned out cars and locomotives of their own, both often a little different than their south-of-the-border contemporaries. Among these were special, Spartan, "Colonist" cars used to transport the flood of European immigrants to their new homesteads in Alberta, Saskatchewan, and the Canadian West. Colonist cars were extremely simple affairs, suitable to the extremely cheap fares charged these immigrants, and they were pulled very slowly across the miles. These modest cars had simple bunks

TRANS-CANADA LIMITED

FASTEST TRAIN ACROSS THE CONTINENT

SLEEPING CARS ONLY

ABOVE: Travel across Canada must have been a lot of fun, even on the fastest trains, when the service was stellar, the scenery amazing, the food impeccable, and with a comfortable little room or sleeper to bunk down in at night. When there was a roomy observation platform at the rear of the train, to sit and talk, and enjoy it all, the ride was a delight.

RIGHT: A good example of a partially streamlined locomotive, this 4-8-4 Northern of the Canadian Pacific flashes its elephant-ear shrouding as it rotates on a turntable.

OPPOSITE: Here comes The Canadian at Morant's Curve in the Bow River Valley. Passenger train travel in Canada's west has always offered spectacular scenery, and has normally been accompanied by superior accommodations and service, too.

but lacked any bedding. Immigrant passengers cooked for themselves in these simple Second Class coaches.

But for First Class travelers—and for the tourist class hungry for a look at the many wonders of the Canadian West—glorious sleeping cars and diner cars were available. The Canadian Pacific Railway offered elegant travel on its Imperial Limited, starting in June 1899, on a run between Montreal and Vancouver. The trip was scheduled for one hundred hours and the service was daily. The Imperial Limited included the required baggage car followed by one or two deluxe Palace sleeping cars, one tourist sleeper, and a dining car.

The heavy tourist trade prompted some Canadian railroads operating in the far west to add open-air observation cars at the end of the train. These cars could accommodate fifty or so passengers on simple bench seats, out in the breeze and sun, where they could marvel at the rugged Canadian Rockies.

Canada has its own revered railroad history, complete with names not always familiar in the United States—Soo Line, Grand Trunk, Canadian Pacific, Canadian Northern, Intercolonial, and others. Six of Canada's major railroads were combined in 1919 to form Canadian National, the dominant railroad in the dominion.

THE BUDD COMPANY

Manufacturers of automobile bodies, frames, wheel assemblies and brakes. Builders of stainless steel trains and highway trailers. Advanced engineering and research. A United States Defense resource.

GREAT DOMES ON THE GREAT NORTHERN

The Great Northern Railway is an engineering masterpiece blessed by some of the most wonderful scenery in America.

Its Empire Builder glides past towering Rocky Mountains in Glacier National Park . . . along jade rivers and white-capped Puget Sound . . . through the forested Cascades . . . on its super-scenic trail between Chicago, St. Paul-Minneapolis, Spokane, Seattle and Portland.

Here are sights to thrill you, watching through the enormous curved windows of the new stainless steel dome cars, built by Budd, which now distinguish the Great Northern's Empire Builder.

The Great Northern, in company with many other railroads, has made every imaginative provision to make your trip by train the most restful, the most stimulating way to travel . . . the safest and most certain way to reach your destination . . . sprinkled all over with enjoyment.

To provide this feast of travel perfection, railroads call on Budd.

Budd

Philadelphia   Detroit   Gary

OPPOSITE: *Cutting through the Rocky Mountains, this Canadian Pacific Railroad freight train approaches Spiral Tunnels near Field, British Columbia.*

ABOVE: *For a scenic trip across the Great White North, you couldn't do much better than a seat in one of the Great Northern's dome cars.*

RIGHT: *This 4-6-2 Pacific class locomotive is relatively new in this 1954 photograph. Steam locomotives were disappearing everywhere in Canada as well as the United States at the time, although many examples soldiered on in low-profile freight service.*

LEFT: *A vintage advertisement for Canadian Pacific.*

ABOVE: *Canadian National's No. 6167 is a Northern-class 4-8-4 blasting across a trestle in October, 1961, during the closing chapter of the age of steam.*

OPPOSITE: *No. 2828 is a streamlined 2-8-2 Mikado of the Canadian Pacific.*

CHAPTER FOUR

OPPOSITE: Fast, clean, and beautiful in a way quite unlike steam locomotives, the GG1 proved to be a huge hit when it began service along the Boston-New York-Washington corridor in the late 1930s.

ABOVE: No. 151 was built by EMD for the Atcheson, Topeka & Santa Fe in 1940. The strength, stamina, and reliability of such diesel power quickly doomed much of the steam fleet to the scrap heap.

THE END OF STEAM

The sudden demise of steam technology was a shock and surprise to many people in America, and is still a source of disappointment and dismay to legions of modern railfans. But it was no surprise to most of the people who ran the railroads. Steam was a wonderful technology in its day, and steam-powered trains were largely responsible for the economic miracle that was the nineteenth-century American economy. But when diesel engines of sufficient size, power, torque range, and efficiency were developed to power mainline locomotives in passenger and freight service, the contest was short and brutal. Steam was theatrical, romantic, musical, and traditional; it was also extremely inefficient in every way—in the amount of fuel converted to drawbar horsepower, in the number of skilled technicians and amount of time needed to service the beasts, and in the frequent stops required by every steam engine to replenish coal and water along the way.

111

ABOVE: While First Class may have been the way to go during the Golden Age of Rail Travel, the new railroads were careful to cater to less wealthy passengers, who could pay less, but came in bigger numbers. Pitching free pillows for coach and chaircar passengers was one way of luring middle class travelers.

RIGHT: An early Union Pacific streamliner.

The New Rails

Diesel engines have been around since 1898 and gasoline four-stroke-cycle engines even longer. Electrification of railroads began in 1888 with street-car lines and soon expanded to mainline operations. Around the time of World War I, experiments were begun to combine the use of an internal combustion engine with electrical drive, first using gasoline engines and later with more efficient and economical diesel. General Electric made a little gasoline-electric unit for an inter-urban line in 1913, and several others over the next five years.

The first railway application of diesel-electric propulsion occurred in Canada, around the time of World War I, followed by small switchers in the United States beginning in 1922. These diesel engines delivered power to the driving wheels in a somewhat novel and seemingly inefficient way, by attachment to an electrical generator wired to motors geared to the wheels.

While puttering around the yards these little switchers demonstrated some talents—low cost of

operation, low cost of maintenance, very high availability rates (since they didn't have to take frequent breaks for water and coal), and a lot of power in a small package. Those early diesels, very much like the ones of today, are mechanically very simple systems; the parts are generally huge, but there aren't a lot of them.

It took some time for all the pieces to come together, but by the early 1930s—despite the depression—several railroads were ready to test the diesel in mainline high-speed passenger operations. The first was Union Pacific with its M10000. The most dramatic and successful was Burlington's Zephyr. Both came out in 1934, and both blew the proverbial doors off the competition.

Only in very recent years has a diesel locomotive been manufactured that could equal the most powerful steam locomotives—but that didn't really matter. Diesel locomotives have long been harnessed together in what train crews call "lash-ups" where multiple locomotives are all controlled by one engineer. Each

of the individual locomotives may be relatively weak, but their combined output can be incredible. This ability to customize the power for a specific train on a specific run was one of the things that helped with the conversion.

The collapse of the steam railroad technology was stunning. In 1930, as diesels began to attract serious attention for mainline service, about 60,000 steam locomotives were being built and put into service every year. That same year seventy-seven gas- or diesel-electrics were sold, and about 660 pure electric locomotives.

By 1940, mostly as a result of the depression, that figure dropped to around 40,000 steam locomotives, 967 diesel-electrics, and 900 pure electrics. Only the drastic transportation demands of World War II postponed the complete conversion from steam to diesel. During the war years, around 900 diesel locomotives of all types were built annually while approximately 40,000 steamers were manufactured. By the 1950s, locomotive builders were pump-

ing out diesels as fast as they could, and at the same time, the railroads were taking cutting torches to nearly new, state of the art steam locomotives—the accountants proved to the railroad corporation officers that, as romantic as steam may have been, steam wasn't nearly as profitable as diesel power, and the railroad technology war was over.

Throughout the decade, between 20,000 and 30,000 diesels hit the rails while steam construction declined to nearly zero—871 in 1959, 374 in 1960, just 210 in 1961, and only 136 in the final year of production, 1962.

LEFT: Quite soon after the M-10000 and Zephyr demonstrated the potential of lightweight, aerodynamically clean, train-sets powered by internal combustion engines instead of steam, these new locomotives began appearing at the front of the nation's premier trains—in this case, the City of Los Angeles, City of Portland, and City of Denver.

The First Streamliner:
Union Pacific's M10000

The depression created both problems and opportunities for individuals and companies. All the railroads saw passenger and freight traffic collapse, starting in 1930, and all were desperate to find ways to revive it. Officers of the Union Pacific (UP), along with those

from the Chicago, Burlington & Quincy (CB&Q), saw demonstrations of several very large General Motors diesels, and both companies began development of new trains to take advantage of the technology. The race was on.

UP's engineering department teamed up with specialists from the Massachusetts Institute of Technology (MIT) to design an entirely new train, based on the GM powerplant and with the Pullman Company fabricating the cars. The design was based

on wind tunnel tests at MIT and was unique, utterly unlike any conventional train of the past. Even more aerodynamically "clean" than airplanes of the time, the whole trainset was designed to slide through the air with a minimum of drag.

UP's design relied heavily on the use of aluminum alloys and construction techniques similar to those used in aircraft. Instead of a heavy frame with a separate body bolted on, UP's design was essentially a single structure of welded metal formed in the shape of a tube. GM didn't have the diesel engine ready in time to beat the CB&Q's entry, so UP installed a four-stroke-cycle distillate engine instead, until the diesel version was finished.

The result was officially called the M10000 but commonly known as the "Streamline Train." The whole trainset weighed just eighty-five tons, less than 10 percent of the weight of a conventional passenger train of 1934, and its 600hp engine could easily power itself down the track at 90 to 120 miles per hour (144.81 to 193.08kph). As originally configured, the M10000 could accommodate 116 passengers plus 22,000 pounds (9,988kg) of baggage and mail. The radical new train was first shown to the public on February 25, 1934.

After its introduction, and before the competing CB&Q locomotive made its debut, UP sent it around the country on a 13,000-mile tour to drum up new business. The distillate engine was soon replaced by a 'proper' diesel. The "Streamlined Train," as it became known, glided into Kansas City's Union Station in April, attracting hordes of spectators for three days, then moved on. It would be back the next year, operating out of Kansas City's Union Station and making a daily round trip to Salina, Kansas, 187 miles (300.88km) each way.

Since its intended operation was for fairly short trips of three or four hours, the Streamlined Train wasn't set up with the elaborate dining cars and Pullman sleepers found on the long-distance runs. But it was intended to provide luxurious travel just the same, and a kitchen and buffet at the end of the train was set up to provide light meals, ice cream, coffee, and similar refreshments between mealtimes.

When it was time for lunch, though, the UP attendants pushed a cart up the aisle and served passengers at their seats from a rolling steam table. Rather than heavy china, their dishes were lightweight plastic ("gaily colored" the brochures of the time said, but probably garish to our tastes today), ostensibly to save weight. This dinner service weighed about 190 pounds (86.26kg) total, much less than the 530 pounds of a ceramic equivalent—and you couldn't break those plates with a hammer.

The windows were all safety glass, an innovation borrowed from the auto industry, and were sealed tight. Air-conditioning kept the whole train cool even in a Kansas August (according to the promotional materials, anyway).

Passengers who had traveled much on the old coaches of previous decades must have thought they'd died and gone to heaven the first time they headed for the lavatory. Instead of the dark and dingy washrooms of an earlier era, UP's Streamline Train had two washrooms in each coach, one at each end of the car, and they were bright, clean, and elegant. Washstands were made of bright metal, and the women's had a big plate-glass mirror and dressing stand.

The trial program took the Streamline Train around much of the nation, through twenty-two states and over fourteen different railroads, up to 8,000 feet (2,438.4m) in the Rockies, through snowstorms, and across California's scorching Mojave Desert.

GM's big diesel was finally installed, a 900hp V-12 brute for the first, followed by 1200hp V-16s for later models. UP was so gratified by the response to the train and demand for seats on it that three special Pullman cars were added to some planned trainsets, each of which was designed and built to blend in nicely with the existing cars. These Pullmans each offered twenty berths in two sections, plus one private compartment and one private bedroom. Some were even designed with 6 inches (15.24cm) extra length for tall passengers, and all of them were enclosed by moveable panels for privacy. The Pullman cars also included private dressing rooms for men and women in each coach. Every Pullman berth on the Streamlined Train even included a little washstand and mirror for bedtime preparations.

The Streamline Train was born in an era of record setting and breaking so it was natural that UP would wind it up and turn it loose to see what it could do in October of 1934 (particularly after its rival's success, described below). UP sent it across the United States, from Los Angeles to New York, a 3,259-mile (5,249.73km) run that was normally eighty-four hours behind the best steam locomotives. The Streamline Train did it in just under fifty-seven hours, more than a whole day faster, and averaged better than 80 miles (128.72km) an hour on the long gradual downhill slope from Cheyenne to Omaha, more than 500 miles (804.5km).

The M10001, as the modified locomotive-trainset was known, did pretty well in revenue service and was the forerunner of thousands of streamlined diesel locomotives and lightweight passenger cars. But its success would soon be eclipsed by another, very similar experiment, the entry by the Chicago, Burlington & Quincy.

OPPOSITE: Union Pacific's M-1000 pioneered the "streamliner" concept with internal combustion power, but it wasn't a diesel. Instead, it was powered by a gasoline powerplant, enclosed in a lightweight body designed with the help of the Massachusetts Institute of Technology. It created a sensation at the Chicago World's Fair, as shown here, in 1934.

ABOVE: With a booming economy and lots of post-war enthusiasm, Americans were ready for vacation. This 1951 UP brochure tried to lure them out on the rails in comfortable, affordable coach cars.

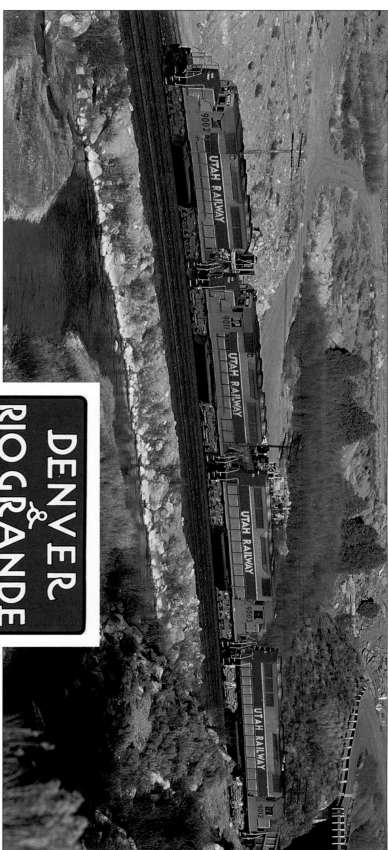

EMD's Beautiful Bulldog

Of all the classics in the long, grand tradition of American passenger railroading, the short list surely includes the sleek and stately locomotives built by General Motor's Electro-Motive Division (EMD). The first went into service in June, 1937, for the Baltimore & Ohio, a design that utterly dominated the market for passenger locomotives for most of its long, profitable life. There were ten variants on the basic design, the most popular of which was the E7.

The E7 was sold right after World War II, from 1945 till 1949. 1,010 A and B units for the E7 were produced, far more than any other model. Total production for all the Es was 1,314 units.

E7s produced 2000hp from twin GM Model 567 12-cylinder diesel engines (although later variants would up that to 2400hp). Depending on how the traction motors were geared, that allowed top speeds of between 98 and 117 miles

SCENIC LINE OF THE WORLD

THRU THE ROCKIES — NOT AROUND THEM

DENVER & RIO GRANDE WESTERN

Royal Gorge Route

VIA HANGING BRIDGE

Royal Gorge of the Arkansas River

ABOVE: A four-unit lash-up of SD-40u locomotives off in search of adventure. One of the great selling points for diesels wasn't their tremendous power, but their ability to be assembled in units like this, all controlled by one engineer from the lead unit.

LEFT: A vintage ad for the Denver & Rio Grande Western.

RIGHT: This is modern railroading in action—extremely powerful, efficient, agile locomotives rapidly moving commodities at very low cost per ton/mile. These hopper cars are making a return trip from a distant powerplant back to be refilled with enough low-sulphur coal to supply the city with electricity for twelve hours or so.

per hour (157.68 and 188.25kph) in theory, though few locomotives ever attain such speeds unless they've just managed to run off a high bridge. The E7s tended to be durable, reliable, locomotives that worked beautifully for many applications, for many years and many miles. Some racked up five or six million miles (8,045,000 or 9,654,000km) and fifteen years or more of revenue service before going off to the locomotive knacker and the cutting torch.

With 1,200 gallons (4,560L) of fuel and 330 gallons (1,254L) of lube oil aboard, the Es were all able to make long runs without servicing. Passenger variants came equipped with feed water heaters and 1,350-gallon (5,130L) tanks to provide steam for the heating system of the consist.

Dynamic brakes were added to later models, a tremendous aid to control a train on a down-slope, where the train is coasting down grade. Dynamic braking turns the traction motor into an electrical generator; instead of using power, the motor produces it. This electrical energy is dissipated in a grid of wires under the hood of the locomotive—a kind of huge toaster on steroids. The effect is to retard the train without the application of the conventional brakes, saving them for more urgent situations.

OPPOSITE: **Central Vermont No. 4559 clatters over the Conrail crossover at Palmer, Massachusetts.**

RIGHT: **Illinois Central Train GLCE glides past downtown Chicago near 18th Street with a mixed freight.**

LEFT: *Santa Fe 108 West at the top of the grade near Church Rock, New Mexico. The locomotive is an EMD GP-60M, built in 1990, with a long load of piggyback trailers in tow.*

OPPOSITE: *While all the EMD locomotives tend to look pretty much alike on the outside, there are all sorts of changes under that tough hide, each with its own model designation. This one is a SD-50, and the SD stands for "Special Duty." Even so, Conrail 6177 is emerging from the woods with a mixed freight near the town of Fort Montgomery, New York.*

The Glittering, Gleaming, GG-1

One of the most stunningly beautiful and impressive locomotives isn't a steamer and isn't a diesel—it is the pure electric drive GG-1 designed and built by the Pennsylvania Railroad.

Electric-drive locomotives have been used for more than a hundred years, and the Pennsy started using them in 1905. They have many advantages over both steam and diesel—they are clean, quiet, simple to maintain, and can be blazingly fast or incredibly powerful. If it were not for the cost of installing and maintaining the electrical transmission lines on which they depend, these locomotives would be in widespread use today.

The GG-1 was part of an electrification program by the Pennsy that began in 1915 in the congested areas around Philadelphia and that extended over the years to the whole New York City to Washington, DC, corridor. The system used a network of overhead wires charged with 11,000 volts of alternating current (AC). Until 1927, this electrified system was used mostly to shuttle passenger trains in and out of the area. The electrical locomotives didn't need to be turned

around at the end of a run but could be used in either direction, a big advantage at the time. But their use was limited and local until Westinghouse developed an improved traction motor for use on locomotives. This new design was small enough to fit between the wheels and still deliver enough power to operate a normal passenger train at high speed.

This innovation encouraged Pennsy to develop electrified mainline passenger locomotives and at the same time to extend the wires all the way from New York City to Washington, DC. Several prototype locomotives were built and tested. There were the normal teething troubles, but by 1934, one proved to be ideal, and it was designated the GG1.

Compared to other locomotives, the GG-1 is a bit of an oddball. It is actually two locomotives in one, back to back. Each of these is what could be called a 4-6-0 format—four unpowered wheels on the leading truck, six larger driving wheels behind, without any trailing truck.

Pennsy bought 139 GG-1s, and there were many variations among them, but here are the basics: the

locomotive was just under 80 feet (24.38m) long, 10 1/2 feet (32m) wide, and 15 feet (4.57m) high (with the pantograph lowered).

The heart of any locomotive is its power delivery system, and on the GG-1 that system was based on twelve traction motors geared directly to the 57-inch (144.78cm) drive wheels. Each of these traction motors were rated at 385hp, a total of 4620 horsepower. Depending on the way these motors were geared, the GG-1 was good for well over 100 miles per hour (106.9kph) and could accelerate to that speed in just over one minute—not bad for a vehicle weighing nearly half a million pounds (227,000kg).

Pennsy ordered fifty-seven of these and divided the order between three sources to speed up delivery—their own shops in Altoona, Pennsylvania, General Electric, and Baldwin Locomotive Works. When the wires were finally in place all the way from New York City to the nation's capital, a shiny new GG-1

OPPOSITE: Most of the 139 GG-1s built for the Pennsy have long since been chopped up and melted down, but sixteen survivors still exist. Because of their specialized electrical components, however, they are even more difficult to restore to running order than steamers, and without the overhead wires to provide power, impossible to move, so all are destined to be static displays.

LEFT: Electric locomotives like the GG-1 would have been a lot more popular if the cost of electrification of their right-of-way hadn't been so high. This GG-1 zooms quietly along in this 1948 photograph between the massive and tremendously expensive power lines required to provide the locomotive with juice.

ABOVE: A vintage advertisement for the Pennsylvania Railroad.

was ready to join in the festivities at Washington's Union Station.

The GG-1 looked unlike other locomotives, partly because of the sleek skin or "carbody" enclosing its systems. Its lines and contours were functional as well as attractive and aerodynamic, designed to enhance visibility for the crew. The placement of the cab well aft was functional, too, intended to help protect the crew in the inevitable grade-crossing encounters with cars and trucks.

Industrial designer Raymond Loewy worked on

the GG-1 and is responsible for the "cat's whisker" pinstripes that embellished the locomotive. Painted in deep Brunswick Green or Tuscan Red, both signature colors of the Pennsy, these gleaming rockets on rails made a lasting impression on several generations of travelers.

GG-1s zoomed up and down the Capital corridor for half a century, surely the champion mainline passenger locomotive in American railroad history. The last were finally retired in the 1980s, and sixteen still survive.

LEFT: *Pennsylvania Railroad No. 4879 is one of 139 similar locomotives, designed in the middle of the depression, and in service for fifty years. Capable of 100mph and blinding acceleration, clean, reliable, and quiet, they were just the ticket for the Boston–New York–Washington corridor for which they were designed.*

ABOVE: *Underneath all that grime is Raymond Loewy's, General Electric's, and Pennsylvania Railroad's beautiful marvel, the GG-1 electric locomotive. It is essentially two ten-wheel locomotives joined at the backbone, and without the need for either diesel engine or boilers, since its electricity comes from wires overhead, it is all power output from one end to the other.*

OPPOSITE: *More than fifty years after its introduction, the GG-1 was still in service when this photograph was made in 1981. That's a tremendously long time for any locomotive, and a testament to the engineering excellence of these fine machines.*

F7 Locomotive

In 1930, when General Motors swallowed up the little diesel-electric builder Electro-Motive Company and Winton, another builder, it was with the express intention of taking over a big slice of the market for internal-combustion-engine/electric locomotive production. The result was GM's Electro-Motive Division and with all those dollars behind it, the new company was quickly a powerhouse. The CB&Q Pioneer Zephyr was its first famous product. A more famous product, the E and F series "Covered Wagon" locomotives, followed.

The Es were designed for passenger service and came equipped with steam generators to heat the cars, electrical generators to light them, and gearing to move them down the track at high velocity. The Fs were essentially the same basic package, without the sissy stuff, and with lower gear ratios that would let them pull freight trains up steep cliffs.

These locomotives were powered by a pair of 900 horsepower V-12 diesels, each cylinder of which displaced 567 cubic inches (1,440.18cm^3)—about double the total displacement of a large car engine. Over the years the engines improved and the specs changed for the Es and Fs, and more than seven thousand sold. They were among the most attractive diesels of all time, and among the most successful, too.

OPPOSITE: The diesel unit at the head of the California Zephyr hauls a consist of passenger cars, including five dome cars.

RIGHT: Long after the "Covered Wagons" had been run off the mainline freights and passenger runs, and when they were still too good for scrap but too beat up for much else, lots of antique F7s were put out to pasture with short consists of commuter chair cars. By this time, their diesel engines had a million or two miles on the meter, and their reliability was not up to old standards—commuters were frequently late when the engines failed.

ABOVE RIGHT: This old "hogger" had some changes to make when he transitioned from steam to diesel. His cockpit is considerably cleaner, quieter, and the visibility is great, but there are a lot of new controls to learn, along with an entirely different way of driving a train. This is the cab of a brand new EMD F unit in the late 1940s or early 1950s.

RIGHT: **EMD E and F** locomotives are called "Covered Wagons" by railfans because of the nicely curved roofline. The handsome lines of these models, while radically different from most of the steam kettles they replaced, may have had something to do with their rapid acceptance by the public. Even after half a century and more, they still look good, even with just a couple of cars full of commuters headed home to Hartford.

ABOVE: Santa Fe No. 218 halts at Summit, California, during the transition period in American railroading, the early 1950s. This freight is powered by what is in essence four separate locomotives, two "A" units complete with cabs and controls, and two "B" units that are only equipped with diesel engines, generators, and traction motors. All four units, though, are controlled by one engineer as if they were a single power unit ...as long as nothing breaks!

RIGHT: F7 locomotives like Southern Pacific No. 6367, a 1949 product of GM's Electro-Motive Division, were purchased by American railroads in huge numbers right after World War II. While not as powerful as an individual steam locomotive of the time, they had many other virtues that made them attractive to railroad management, and to the crews as well.

EMD GP
Locomotive

One of the great classic locomotives of the early diesel age has to be Electro-Motive Division's beautiful ugly duckling, the General Purpose or GP. Known as the "Geep" in the railroad community, this is one of the great success stories of the conversion from steam, an efficient, economical, reliable locomotive that was as plain as a mud fence, but that kept railroads in the black all over the nation.

Geeps introduced what is called a "hood" configuration—a frame supporting the engine, generator, and cab, all enclosed by a hood. This hood has many access panels allowing access to components and a walkway that surrounds the whole locomotive. Earlier "Covered Wagon" locomotives were fully enclosed with a full-width shell, restricting visibility to the rear.

The first Geep, the GP7, used a 1500hp diesel engine, a muscular powerplant for its post–World War II introduction. That power, along with the locomotive's excellent visibility, its ability to run equally well in either direction, plus the capability of the new diesels to be combined in multiple unit "lash-ups," made purchasing agents forget any love they might have had for their old steam-powered flames. Over 9,000 Geeps sold over the years, and are still selling in new and improved variations. They've been used for switching, as road engines for freight and passenger operations, on the mainlines, and on back woods runs for more than fifty years. Late versions like the GP60 are still very popular with engineers, who prefer them over more recent "wide cab" locomotives like the F59PHI, with its uncomfortable desktop-style ergonomics.

OPPOSITE: EMD GP-40s are used for passenger as well as freight consists, as shown here in Washington, DC.

LEFT: The beloved "Geep," here represented by a GP-40-2, rattles over Bellows Falls in Vermont. The GP stands for "General Purpose," a set of functions that the GP has lived up to for all of its long life.

RIGHT: *GP38-2 No. 204, built by General Motors' Electro-Motive Division, crosses Vermont's Cuttingville Trestle with a consist of mixed freight trailing behind.*

OPPOSITE: *Still in modified warbonnet colors, this lash-up of Dash 9s is grinding its way upslope behind SF No. 723, climbing out of Abo Canyon, New Mexico.*

ABOVE: *Heat shimmers off the top of CNW's No. 8672 outside Dekalb, Illinois, as the Dash 2 hauls a freight train behind it headed west.*

Hotshots and Dog Locals

Running trains across both the U.S. and Canada today is just as exciting and just as important as ever. Priority trains like the QNYLA get the best power and the open blocks. You can watch them blasting across Missouri, Kansas, down into New Mexico, and westbound through Arizona with their long strings of "double-stacks" rushing from coast to coast.

The power on the point will be the million-dollar wonders. The SD90MACs, the AC4400s—all the amazing new computer-controlled, air-conditioned machines in their five and six-unit lash-ups don't have the flash and thunder of steam, but they have a charm and grace of their own.

LEFT: Here comes the "hotshot" fast freight known as TVLA at Bear Mountain, New York, a priority train running across the country at high speed behind power furnished by Conrail. At Chicago, the name changes to QNYLA —the Q is for "quality" and the NYLA is for the origin and destination of the hotshot: New York and Los Angeles—pulled by Santa Fe locomotives.

OPPOSITE: Conrail No. 5566 hauls a train of containerized freight near Bear Mountain, New York.

Dash Nine Locomotive

General Electric now produces one of the most popular contemporary diesel locomotives, the Dash 9-44CW. First produced in 1993, many hundreds have been sold. They are among the most common modern locomotives running the rails today. Railroads like Santa Fe bought them in large quantities, starting in 1993, and Santa Fe (now Burlington Northern Santa Fe) has picked up the tab for over six hundred as of this writing. As with almost any locomotive model, variations are common in specifications, but here are the basics for the big Dash 9: The engine is a turbocharged, monstrous sixteen-cylinder 7FDL engine capable of producing up to 4,400 horsepower and can apply 140,000 pounds (63,560kg) of pull at the drawbar to its trailing load. That's twice as much as locomotives of the recent past, and just the thing for those long strings of coal cars.

Dash 9s are widecabs just over 73 feet (22.25m) long and weigh 392,000 pounds (177,968kg) fueled—and that includes 5,000 gallons (19,000L) of diesel fuel, 380 gallons (1,444L) of coolant, plus 410 gallons (1,558L) of lube oil. Besides all that, Dash 9s carry 40 cubic feet (12.19m^3) of sand for traction. Like all contemporary locomotives, the Dash 9 relies heavily on computer controls to govern things like fuel flow and to diagnose faults.

OPPOSITE: More trailers headed west, but only part way behind CNW No. 8622 West, seen here gliding below another coaling tower designed for locomotives of a different breed, this one at Nelson, Illinois.

RIGHT: Burlington Northern sucked up the legendary Santa Fe and railfans have been bawling in their rootbeer ever since. BN has introduced all sorts of new technologies and engines, but the loss of Santa Fe's bright red and yellow for BN's pumpkin-colored power is, for some, just too much to accept.

OPPOSITE: *BNSF No. 9899 East with a string of coal cars.*

ABOVE: *January in Illinois is a tough time to run a train or make photographs of one. Canadian National No. 2509 is on BNSF trackage here at Lee, Illinois.*

ABOVE: *Burlington Northern hauls a lot of coal from Wyoming to a lot of power-plants around the Midwest, and they haul most of it with new alternating-current locomotives like this SD70MAC. The exterior is conventional but beneath that long hood lurks a new technology that allows two new locomotives to do the work of three old ones.*

RIGHT: *A pair of Conrail SD80MACs with a mixed freight.*

OPPOSITE: *CNW 8652 West rolls past Geneva, Illinois, at sunset with a rather short mixed freight.*

SD70MAC
Locomotive
and Beyond

Today's railroads are still inventing the artform with new technologies and new ways of moving cargoes down the line. During the 1990s, that involved alternating current instead of DC and engine output up to 6,000hp. The first AC locomotive was EMD's SD70MAC, an extremely powerful model that could replace four conventional locomotives hauling coal trains for Burlington Northern (BN).

Early SD70MACs were so impressive that BN ordered 350 with one signature, then another eighty-four soon after. These engines don't look a lot different on the outside from many locomotives on the rails, but their performance has transformed the industry. Their tractive effort—their ability to exert force on the drawbar—is much greater than conventional DC locomotives with the same

4,000hp diesels, resulting in fewer AC locomotives doing the same work of larger numbers of DC units—three ACs typically replace five DCs.

As if that wasn't good enough, EMD bumped up the power of the engines to 5,000hp with the SD80MAC and to 6,000hp with the SD90MAC. This latter locomotive is sure to be a classic of the future—it can easily rip the couplers right off the trailing load with its 200,000 pounds (90,800kg) of rated starting tractive power.

Suggested Reading

Beebe, Lucius, and Charles M. Clegg. *Mixed Train Daily.* New York: E.P. Dutton, 1947.

Beebe, Lucius. *20th Century.* Berkeley, California: Howell-North, 1962.

——. *Mr Pullman's Elegant Palace Car: The Railway Carriage That Established a New Dimension of Luxury and Entered the National Lexicon as a Symbol of Splendor.* Garden City, New York: Doubleday, 1961.

Flinchum, Russell. *Henry Dreyfuss, Industrial Designer: The Man in the Brown Suit.* New York: Rizzoli, 1997.

Frew, Tim. *Locomotives: From the Steam Locomotive to the Bullet Train.* New York: Michael Friedman Publishing Group, 1990.

Garratt, Colin. *Steam Trains: A World Portrait.* London: Tiger Books International, 1989.

Glischinski, Steve. *Burlington Northern and Its Heritage.* Andover, New Jersey: Andover Junction Publications, 1992.

Halberstadt, Hans. *Working Steam: Vintage Steam Locomotives Today.* New York: Michael Friedman Publishing Group: 2000.

Halberstadt, April, and Hans Halberstadt. *Great American Train Stations: Classic Terminals and Depots.* New York: Barnes & Noble Publishers, 1997.

——. *Santa Fe Railway.* Osceola, Wisconsin: Motorbooks International, 1997.

Holbrook, Stewart H. *The Story of American Railroads.* New York: Alfred A. Knopf, 1955.

Hubbard, Freeman. *Great Trains of All Time.* New York: Grosset & Dunlap, 1962.

Husband, J. *The Story of the Pullman Car.* New York: McGraw-Hill, 1946.

Mulhearn, Daniel J., and John R. Taibi. *General Motors F-Units: The Locomotives That Revolutionized Railroading.* New York: Quadrant Press Inc., 1982.

Riley, C.J. *The Encyclopedia of Trains and Locomotives.* New York: Michael Friedman Publishing Group: 2000.

Schafer, Mike. *Classic American Railroads.* Osceola, Wisconsin: Motorbooks International, 1996.

Schafer, Mike. *Vintage Diesel Locomotives.* Osceola, Wisconsin: Motorbooks International, 1998.

Shafer, Mike, and Joe Welsh. *Classic American Streamliners.* Osceola, Wisconsin: Motorbooks International, 1997.

Solomon, Brian, with C.J. Riley. *Along the Rails: The Lore and Legend of the Railroad.* New York: MetroBooks, 2000.

Stegmaier, Harry. *Southern Pacific Passenger Train Consists and Cars: 1955–58.* Austin, Texas: TLC Graphics, 2001.

Stevenson, Robert Louis. *Across the Plains.* New York: Charles Scribner's Sons, 1897.

Tretiack, Philippe. *Universe of Style: Raymond Loewy and Streamlined Design.* Np: Universe Publishing, 1999.

Weaver, John C. *The American Railroads.* Garden City, New York: Doubleday, 1958.

Welsh, Joseph M. *By Streamliner, New York to Florida.* Andover, New Jersey: Andover Junction Publications, 1994.

Zimmerman, Karl R. *The Remarkable GG1.* New York: Quadrant Press, 1977.

Resources

The Best Friend of Charleston Museum
456 King Street
Charleston, South Carolina 29403
(843) 973-7269
www.charleston.net/org/railroad

Burlington Route Historical Society
Membership Services, Dept. I
P.O. Box 456
La Grange, Illinois 60525
www.burlingtonroute.com

California State Railroad Museum
111 "I" Street
Sacramento, California 95814
(916) 445-6645
www.californiastaterailroadmuseum.org.

The Golden Gate Railroad Museum
Hunter's Point Naval Shipyard
San Francisco, California
(415) 822-8728
www.ggrm.org

Illinois Railway Museum
P.O. Box 427
Union, Illinois 60180
(800) BIG-RAIL
www.irm.org

Mad River & NKP Railroad Society, Inc.
233 York Street
Bellevue, Ohio 44811-1377
(419) 483-2222
www.onebellevue.com/madriver

The National Museum of Transportation
3815 Barrett Station Road
St. Louis, Missouri 63122
(314) 965-6885.
www.museumoftransport.org

National New York Central Railroad Museum
721 South Main St.
Elkhart, Indiana 46515
219-294-3001

National Railway Historical Society
P.O. Box 58547
Philadelphia, Pennsylvania 19102
www.nrhs.com

The Pioneer Zephyr Exhibit
at the Museum of Science and Industry, Chicago
57th Street and Lake Shore Drive,
Chicago, Illinois 60637
(773) 684.1414
www.msichicago.org

The Railroad Museum of Pennsylvania
Railroad Museum of Pennsylvania
P. O. Box 15
Strasburg, Pennsylvania 17579
www.rrmuseumpa.org

Photo Credits

©Howard Ande: pp. 1, 117, 118, 119, 120, 121, 127 bottom, 128, 132, 133 left, 134, 135, 136, 138, 139, 141

Brown Brothers: pp. 6-7, 13, 14 left, 15, 17, 22, 44, 45, 46, 47 top, 51 top, 53, 54, 57 left, 57 right, 58-59, 59 right, 64 top, 64 bottom, 65 top, 67, 68 top, 74, 75, 85, 110, 112 bottom, back end papers

Courtesy of Russell Colegrove: pp. 14 right, 32 right, 55 bottom, 56 top, 58 top left, 58 center left, 58 bottom left, 62 bottom, 63 left, 63 top, 63 bottom, 65 top right, 71 right, 87 right, 89 right, 91 top, 91 bottom, 86 top, 98 left, 112 left, 115, 116 center

Canadian Pacific Railway Archives: pp. 104 left, 104 right, 105, 106, 108 left, 109

Burlington Route Historical Society: pp. 20 top, 38 bottom, 61, 62 top, 92, 97, 98, 99 left, 99 right, 100 top, 126, 127 top

Corbis: p. 77

Steven Cryan: pp. 43, 94 bottom

Illinois State Historical Library: p. 93, 101

Kansas State Historical Society: p. 82 top left

David Lotz Collection: p. 25 bottom

M.D. McCarter Collection: pp. 9, 16, 19, 25 top, 27, 29 bottom, 32 left, 39 bottom, 41 bottom, 49, 51 bottom, 52, 56 bottom, 76 bottom, 81, 83 left, 96 bottom, 114, 123 bottom, 124 bottom, 129 top

New York Central System Historical Society: pp. 47 bottom, 50, 70, 73

Private Collection: p. 78

©Brian Solomon: pp. 5, 12, 23, 24, 40, 65, 80, 89 left, 93 top, 94 top, 122, 137, 140 bottom, 142

©Richard Jay Solomon: p. 76 top

Superstock: pp. 72, 95

©Al Tillotson: pp. 125, 130, 131, 133 right, 140 top

Courtesy of Kevin Ullrich: pp. 30 top, 39 top, 68 bottom, 102

©H. L. Vail: p. 33

©Jay Williams: pp. 42, 86, 87, 90, 116 top

Jay Williams Collection: pp. 2, 8, 10 bottom, 10-11, 11 bottom, 18, 20 bottom, 21, 26 bottom, 28 bottom, 28-29, 30 bottom, 31 bottom, 34, 35 top left, 35 top right, 36 bottom, 36 top, 37, 38 top, 41 top, 48, 55 left, 60 top, 60 bottom, 66 left, 69, 79 bottom, 82 right, 83 right, 84 bottom, 88, 100 bottom, 107 bottom, 108 right, 111, 113, 124 top, 129 bottom, front end papers

Courtesy of Michael Zega: pp. 71 top left, 79 top, 84 left, 88 left, 103, 107 inset, 123 right